Rule of Terror

Stalin as a young man

Rule of Terror

Russia under Lenin and Stalin

Hellmut Andics

Translated by Alexander Lieven

HOLT, RINEHART AND WINSTON

New York   Chicago   San Francisco

Acknowledgements

The author and publishers are indebted to the following for permission to reproduce copyright material: Messrs. Hamish Hamilton (*The God that failed*, edited by R. H. S. Crossman; extracts from the late André Gide's writings on Russia, translated by Dr. Enid Starkie; *Conspiracy of Silence* by Alexander Weissberg); Messrs. Hamish Hamilton and Messrs. Curtis Brown (*I was Stalin's agent* by Walter A. Krivitsky); Messrs. William Heinemann and Opera Mundi (*Listen Comrades* by Valentin Gonzalez—*El Campesino*); Messrs. Doubleday & Co. (*Lenin* by David Shub); Messrs. William Collins Sons & Company (*Child of the Revolution* by Wolfgang Leonhard); Messrs. Eyre & Spottiswoode (*The Anarchists* by James Joll); Messrs. Thames and Hudson (*Three who made a Revolution* by Bertram D. Wolfe); Messrs. Frederick A. Praeger (*History of Soviet Russia* by Georg von Rauch); Messrs. Cassell & Company (*The Second World War* by Winston S. Churchill); Messrs. Weidenfeld & Nicolson Ltd. (*Tito Speaks* by Vladimir Dedijer); Messrs. Harcourt, Brace & World (*Conversations with Stalin*).

Contents

Author's Preface

THIS is a book about the most cruel experiment in history, an experiment designed to transform the world into an earthly paradise in accordance with the theories of a handful of ideologists. The result was an attempt to rule at first a political party, then a whole State and finally half the globe by brute force, to the exclusion of every basic human right. Any study of this Great Terror must stand back from whatever is purely subjective or transitory in the story, or is tainted with predetermined attitudes towards subjects such as Cold War and Peaceful Co-existence. This is particularly important because the concepts of Marxism and Communism, Bolshevism and Stalinism have altered in very confusing ways during the fifty years since the October Revolution.

This book does not merely catalogue acts of cruelty; the cases quoted are no more than illustrations. *Rule of Terror* sets out to be a living study of violence as an instrument of power. It is an attempt to discover the seeds of this violence in Leninist thought and to trace its fulfilment in the hellish practice of Stalinism.

The author wishes to thank Dr. Christian Broda, the former Austrian Minister of Justice, who suggested the subject of this book; also Margarete Buber-Neumann of Frankfurt and Herman Achimov of Munich for their invaluable advice; and the Institute for the Study of the U.S.S.R. in Munich, whose members made it possible to draw upon a wealth of original material.

Introduction

THE curtain fell on 27th June 1953. It fell that night after a gala performance of *The Decembrists* at Moscow's Bolshoi Theatre. The top political leaders of the Soviet Union were present in the audience. The new collective leadership, headed by Prime Minister Malenkov, was relaxing and showing the world and the Soviet people its genial solidarity. Anyone going to the trouble of counting heads, however, would have been struck by the absence of a man who according to Kremlin protocol had no business to be missing. There was no trace in the Government box of the broad, bald head of the Minister of Internal Affairs, First Deputy Chairman of the Council of Ministers of the U.S.S.R., and Member of the Praesidium of the Central Committee of the Communist Party of the Soviet Union, Lavrenti Pavlovich Beria.

There was a certain tension in the air in Moscow during those last days of June. From time to time, tanks appeared in the streets. Troop carriers patrolled the capital, and the troops were from the Moscow garrison, not units of the State Security Service as one might have expected in connection with some domestic upheaval. Such facts were promptly noted by the experts at the foreign diplomatic missions who had over the years developed a sharp eye for fine distinctions of this kind. The soldiers were most active in the vicinity of the MVD building, in other words the Ministry of Internal Affairs, and around the barracks of the State Security troops.

There seemed to be no obvious reason for these activities. The popular rising of 17th June, when Soviet armour had crushed the mass protest of East German workers, had come and gone ten days earlier. Only later was it apparent that a certain connection did exist between the East German rising and the events in Moscow.

Lavrenti Beria, who had been missing at the gala performance in the Bolshoi Theatre, was not mentioned the following day by *Pravda* in its account of the cultural event held in the presence of the highest dignitaries of the Party and State. In theory, Beria should have been listed between Malenkov and Molotov. It was the pedantic precision of such lists which enabled Western experts to divine with a fair degree of accuracy the relative positions of individuals in the top Soviet leadership and sudden changes in their standing.

The absence of Beria's name therefore gave grounds for speculation, particularly in conjunction with the troop movements around the headquarters of the State Security Service. And it was in fact during those days that the curtain also fell on the career of the Minister of Internal Affairs.

Beria had come into the limelight in 1938. He made his reputation during the Revolution and the Civil War as one of the most active Bolshevist fighters in the Caucasus, traditionally Russia's most unruly territory. He was thirty-nine when Stalin appointed his Georgian compatriot People's Commissar for Internal Affairs.

For a long time the world at large failed to take note of Beria. He usually affected the plainest of plain clothes, even after he had climbed to the highest military rank. With his pince-nez he did not in the least look like a dangerous revolutionary, but rather like a subordinate and dependable book-keeper, modestly lower-middle class.

The figures in his books represented corpses. When fate overtook him in 1953 this man had sat for all of fifteen years at the controls of an infernal machine designed to summon death at the push of a button – a button with Beria's finger on it.

At that time the machinery's official title was MVD, the Ministry of Internal Affairs. The names had often changed. NKVD had been another. In the course of years it had undergone many re-organisations, but the task had remained the same throughout. Two names, long vanished from Soviet official use but firmly etched into the mind of the outside world, summed up the story – Cheka and GPU; they represented a machine for the application of terror to two hundred million Soviet citizens, faultlessly organised down to the smallest detail and stretching to the remotest corner of this gigantic empire.

On 27th June 1953 the man who had steered the machine vanished without a trace from public view. It was only made known many weeks later that the Praesidium of the Supreme

Soviet had decreed his dismissal on 26th June. And the standard list of sins, which unfailingly came into use whenever one of the great in the Kremlin toppled, was now published.

Beria was, all of a sudden, an agent of 'foreign espionage circles', and what is more had been so since 1919, so the bemused citizens of the Soviet Union were informed. The man who during fifteen years had uncovered hundreds of alleged 'conspiracies' and had delivered countless 'conspirators' to the executioner, suddenly became the head of a ring bent on bringing about 'the downfall of Soviet power and the re-introduction of Capitalism'. The Georgian who only a few years earlier had launched a deadly wave of terror over his own homeland was now accused of 'bourgeois nationalist deviations' and indicted of an attempt 'to disrupt the friendship between the peoples of the U.S.S.R.'

These were no more than the formal phrases which reappeared with every purge. Another in the list of Beria's sins was probably nearer the mark: he had attempted, so it was stated, to put the Ministry of Internal Affairs above Party and State, and to use the organs of State Security against the Party and its leadership and against the Government of the U.S.S.R. That was the real indictment: Lavrenti Pavlovich Beria dominated the machine. Such a man had to go. The 'Apparat' of the State Security Service had made Stalin's rule possible; now Beria might have used it to become a new Stalin. His chances of success would have been far greater than those of any other member of the new collective leadership who did not have such an organisation at his disposal.

By getting rid of Beria, Stalin's successors rid themselves of a suffocating fear. It was as though a tacit understanding had been reached between all concerned to do away with the threat of the pistol shot in the back of the neck before the struggle for power could be allowed to proceed. Since nobody could tell during those early months after Stalin's death who would emerge as the winner in the struggle for Stalin's inheritance, new rules of the game were drawn up by mutual consent, and the only competitor who commanded the means of breaking these rules was eliminated. All agreed to safeguard at least the lives of the future losers. The purges of later years proved this point: the vanquished of Khrushchev's era were no longer liquidated – they were merely made powerless, and displaced. The 'enemies of the Party' were not converted into corpses but merely became directors of electric power stations, as in the case of Malenkov, second-rate delegates to atomic authorities, as in that of Molotov, or simply pensioners, like Khrushchev himself.

When 1,355 voting and 81 consulting delegates met on 14th February 1956 for the Twentieth Congress of the Communist Party of the Soviet Union, the programme of the Congress included for the final day, 25th February, a mass meeting in Moscow's Red Square. On 24th February, the mass meeting was cancelled; instead, the delegates were summoned to a closed session. On the agenda was a secret address by the Secretary-General of the Party, Nikita Khrushchev, with a seemingly innocuous title: 'The Personality Cult and Its Consequences.' (Khrushchev's so-called 'secret speech' was first published by the State Department on 4th June 1956. No text has been officially published in the Soviet Union, but neither has there been any attempt to denounce versions published in the West as forgeries.)

It was later said that on hearing the extraordinary revelations made by Khrushchev on that day a number of delegates fainted with excitement. Anastas Mikoyan described the Twentieth Congress as the most important since Lenin. This was no exaggeration. In fact, Khrushchev had drawn up a provisional balance of the entire twenty-nine years since Lenin's death, during which Stalin had ruled the Soviet Union. For the first time he gave the Terror its real name. He spoke of 'intolerance', 'the gross misuse of power' and brutal 'arbitrariness'. He ascribed to the dead dictator 'arrogance', 'megalomania' and 'dedication to self'. Finally, he diagnosed a 'persecution mania' that had 'grown beyond all measure'.

Khrushchev also quoted figures. He did not, let it be said, enumerate the millions of Stalin's dead; he confined himself to facts about liquidations in the upper ranks of the Party. Yet these figures alone might well have given individual delegates occasions to faint if they reflected on the fate that might well have been theirs in the past. Out of 139 members and candidate members, for example, elected to the Central Committee by the Seventeenth Party Congress in 1934, no less than ninety-six were later executed. 1,108 out of 1,966 delegates met again in prison.

When Khrushchev rendered this account the last blood bath already lay some three years in the past. It had engulfed those who

until then had themselves directed the Terror – Beria and his
closest collaborators. They were sentenced to death by a Special
Tribunal at the end of 1953. In the proper Stalinist tradition
physical liquidation was followed by moral anathema, and
Lavrenti Pavlovich Beria's name was erased from the records.
The operation had its comic side. Volume twenty-one of the
Great Soviet Encyclopædia was just being sent to subscribers, and
the parcel included an instruction to cut out pages 21, 22 and 23
– Beria's biography – from Volume Five.

New pages were to be pasted in place of the old, including
pictures of the Bering Sea.

Nearly three years had to pass after Beria's fall until Khrushchev
had sufficiently secured his position to dare to start dismantling
the Terror at the Twentieth Party Congress. In presenting his
dreadful account, Nikita Khrushchev found a curious answer to
the question of how things could have been allowed to go so far:

> Stalin was convinced that all this was necessary for the defence of
> the interests of the working class against the designs of the enemy
> and the attacks of the Imperialist camp. He saw this from the point of
> view of the working class, of the interests of the labouring people, of
> the victory of Socialism and Communism. We must not say that
> these were the deeds of a giddy despot. He considered that this should
> be done in the interest of the Party, of the working masses, in the
> name of the defence of the achievements of the Revolution. In this
> lies the whole tragedy.

But there was one thing which Khrushchev did not do in these
moments of truth on 25th February 1956 – he did not abjure the
use of terror as a legitimate instrument of power. On the contrary,
he said: 'Stalin used the Party and the NKVD for the exercise of
Mass Terror at a time when the class of exploiters had already
been destroyed in our country and there were therefore no
serious reasons for the application of an extraordinary Mass
Terror.'

Thick volumes have been written about the background and
the motives of Khrushchev's admissions at the Twentieth Party
Congress. Yet terror as a means of eliminating an opponent,
violence as a legitimate method of politics remained untouched,
at least in theory. It was merely held in reserve, in case of need,
with or without Stalin, whenever 'serious grounds' existed.

Beria had no successor with comparable powers, but he was

given successors. The State Security Service no longer functions today with the unchecked self-sufficiency and perfection of power at the touch of a button, as in the past the Cheka, the GPU and the NKVD. But a well organised machine remains in being in the shape of the KGB, the Committee for State Security. And the very first Congress since de-Stalinisation, the Twenty-first Congress of 1959, explicitly passed the resolution 'That the Organs of State Security, which must be primarily directed against the agents infiltrated by the Imperialist States, are to be strengthened.'

Mass Terror cannot be spelt out in terms of Stalin only. Stalin did not invent it. Mass Terror in the Communist camp is as old as the Bolshevik Party itself. Its role was first formulated fifty-six years before the Twentieth Party Congress on Christmas Eve of 1900. It was then that the spark was struck that was to become an all-consuming fire.

Part One

THE SPARK

CHAPTER ONE

The Ideology of Violence

As the peace of Christmas was about to settle on the world in 1900, the presses in a small printing works in Leipzig ran just once more for a small edition of the first number of a new periodical. It was called *Iskra* – The Spark. The first copies were delivered on 24th December, but the date of publication was 11th December, because the periodical was printed in Russian, and in 1900 the Russian calendar lagged thirteen days behind the remainder of Europe.

Tzarist Russia lagged behind the remainder of Europe not only by these thirteen calendar days but by decades, and in some respects by centuries. The aim of the new publication was to close this gap by the use of force. The opening article sketched out a programme:

> Do not merely organise yourselves into mutual aid societies, strike funds and workers' circles, organise yourselves also as a political party, organise yourselves for the close struggle against autocratic government and against the whole of capitalist society. Without such an organisation the proletariat is not capable of rising to a conscious class struggle, without such an organisation the workers' movement is condemned to impotence and the working class will never succeed by means of mere strike funds, circles and mutual aid societies in carrying out the great historical task that is incumbent upon it: to free itself and the whole Russian people from political and economic slavery.

The author of this inflammatory appeal had come to Leipzig at the beginning of December to supervise the printing of the first number of the new periodical.

He was at the time living in Munich in a modest rented room under the innocuous name of Meyer. Yet he spoke clumsy German with an unmistakable Russian accent. His egg-shaped head – with dark slit eyes in a Mongoloid face – and his sparse beard also suggested an Asian origin.

In fact, this unusual looking man carried a valid passport in his real name: Vladimir Ilyich Ulyanov, born 10th April 1870, in Simbirsk on the Volga.

Ulyanov had left Russia on 29th July 1900 after three years of exile in Siberia, with sixteen hundred roubles in cash, and a few apparently harmless papers. Given the proper treatment, notes written in secret ink would have been revealed between the lines. In the course of his exile, Ulyanov had successfully graduated from that good school of clandestine and conspiratorial activity – a term of forced residence in Siberia.

The Tzarist police arrested Ulyanov in Petersburg, just before his departure abroad but soon let him go again and, for reasons of their own, left him both his passport and his money.

The sixteen hundred roubles had been provided by Alexandra Kalmykova, a teacher and publisher, the wife of a higher civil servant. Kalmykova's friends called her 'Aunty' and some of these friends had added out of their own pockets to Aunty's contribution. They were determined to help a former exile, in a sense paying conscience money to make up for their service under a tyrannical system. The money was intended for the foundation of *Iskra*.

Its motto had been chosen when Ulyanov was still in Siberia: 'From the spark will spurt the flame.' The plans for its publication had been made in Petersburg: active preparations began when Ulyanov met Vera Zasulich, at the time a living symbol of Anarchist terrorism.

Looking back, we can see that with *Iskra* there was born a Terror which no longer had anything in common with Anarchism, a Mass Terror which would not merely destroy, but would aim to set up by force a Utopian paradise on earth. It was a Terror which would first swamp Tzarist Russia and then flood the whole Eastern hemisphere, a tidal wave of horror, of deportations, of mass executions, of the extermination of entire classes and of genocide covering whole areas of history.

Two godmothers bearing gifts stood at the side of Vladimir Ilyich Ulyanov, the father of this Terror – the former Anarchist Vera Zasulich with ideas and the teacher Alexandra Kalmykova with money. They made a strange pair: Vera Zasulich had devoted her entire youth to terrorism, and the good Aunty Kalmykova hoped that *Iskra* would prove a step towards the liberation of oppressed mankind.

Kalmykova already knew Ulyanov. She had published a book written by him during his years of exile in Siberia. The work appeared under the pseudonym of Vladimir Ilyin. The author seldom made use of his real name after he had left Russia. First he used the pseudonym Ilyin in the newspaper articles and the pamphlets which he published as an émigré, then adopted the name of 'Lenin' some time after he had left Russia.

The encounter between Vera Zasulich and Vladimir Ilyich Lenin at the turn of the century was a meeting of the old and the new generation of the Russian underground. Zasulich was then forty-nine, an untidy looking woman who had already spent nearly quarter of a century as an émigré suffering from acute nostalgia, first in Switzerland, then in England. A typical bohemian, she eked out her existence in a miserable rented room, an intellectual helpless in the face of ordinary life.

Lenin's wife, Nadezhda Krupskaya, tells in her Memoirs how she saw Vera Zasulich belabouring the meat which she was cooking on a camp stove with the same pair of scissors which she used to cut articles from newspapers.

Vera Zasulich was a legendary figure in Russia. As a sixteen-year-old student she was already a friend of the dreaded Anarchist Nechaev. In 1878 she became an active Anarchist herself. She attempted to assassinate General Trepov, the Petersburg Chief of Police, who was loathed for his brutality. The attempt failed. The evidence however was so clear that the Tzarist authorities took the risk of putting the case to a jury. This proved most injudicious. Although there were officials and officers among the jury, the trial turned into a demonstration against the prosecution. The Tzarist regime had become personified in General Trepov and Zasulich, because she tried to assassinate him, became a national heroine. The jury acquitted her. The crowds massed before the court to cheer her and her judges. The police, who had intended to re-arrest the girl, were forced to retreat empty-handed. A second arrest of the young Anarchist would simply have produced a riot. Vera Zasulich fled into exile in Western Europe. Shortly before his death she was in contact with Karl Marx. In 1883 she became one of the founder members of the first Marxist émigré organisation, the 'League for the Liberation of Labour', together with Georgi Valentinovich Plekhanov, the son of a noble landowner, and the former carpenter Pavel Borisovich Axelrod.

The meeting with Vera Zasulich during her secret visit to Russia in 1900 took Lenin into that world of terrorism which he had already come to know only too well during his student days.

His elder brother, Alexander Ulyanov, had belonged to an Anarchist group which had at the beginning of 1887 planned an attempt to murder Tzar Alexander III. The attempt failed, and Alexander Ulyanov was arrested and executed. This conspiracy was the last manifestation of the Anarchist wave of terrorism that had begun with Vera Zasulich's attempt against General Trepov. Not even the fact that the father of the Ulyanov brothers had risen through long service to the post of Director of all public schools in the Province of Simbirsk and had been granted titles of nobility could secure a pardon for Alexander. Nor did his father's influence prevent the dismissal of Vladimir Ilyich from Kazan University, in his very first year of law studies, for participation in a student demonstration. The future Lenin had to continue his studies privately and obtain special permission to sit for his final law examinations as an external student. Thus the future founder of the Bolshevists entered politics direct from a world of violence and bloodshed.

In recent Russian history a direct road leads from Nihilism and Anarchism to Stalinism. Further back, violence and cruelty are part of the foundation of every system of government in Russia, and the people have been well schooled in bearing the consequences. The struggle to fashion the first Russian State, which began in Kiev and continued from Moscow, the Mongol pressure from the East and the Polish pressure from the West, the Swedish campaigns of conquest – all these put individual Russian communities into a state of siege for long periods. Survival often became a matter of competing in cruelty. Add to this the Mir, the communal ownership of land by the villagers, through which every father became the absolute master in his family, and the Council of Elders – the tyrant of the village.

This system turned the landowner into a father figure, giving him power of life and death over the peasants. It made the Tzar, 'the little Father', into an absolute ruler over his subjects: 'Supreme and unlimited power rests in the hands of the Tzar of all the Russias. God commands that his orders should be obeyed not

through fear only, but also following the voice of conscience.'[1]
The ordinary man had come to regard this pyramid of oppression
as the order of things willed by God. When the Revolution of
October 1917 put the Red Tzar in the Kremlin, in place of the
Autocrat of All the Russias, the great mass of the Russian people
did not have to learn new ways.

From 1789 the great European revolutionary movements had
been kept away from Russian territory. The Russians had, willy-
nilly, been forced to slumber through the revolutionary years of
1830 and 1848. Until the twentieth century there were no legal
political parties or any stirrings of parliamentarianism in the
country, and so the accumulated discontent which could find no
outlet exploded into terrorism.

Dostoevsky and Turgenev have traced for us this world in
which Anarchism and Nihilism ran riot. It is a measureless
picture of bitter poverty and hopelessness in a vast landscape
where chill loneliness, born of the long snowbound winter nights,
permeates even the brightest summer day. From this background in which man seems damned to all eternity, Anarchism
emerged as a desperate resolve to destroy that which could not
be improved, in the belief that the essential goodness of man
would make possible a fresh start after the total devastation of
the old order. This is the background of Sergei Nechaev's act
of faith: 'The revolutionary knows only one science – that of
destruction. For its sake, and only for its sake, does he study
mechanics, physics, chemistry and even medicine. For him there
exists only one pleasure, one consolation, one reward, one
satisfaction – the reward of revolution. Day and night he can
allow himself only one thought, only one aim, that of irreparable
destruction. . . .'[2] The revolution sanctified all means according
to Nechaev – poison, dagger and rope.

This is the world of the key figures of Russian literature,
Turgenev's Nezhdanov as well as Dostoevsky's Raskolnikov.
They are not proletarians, since an urban proletariat was only
then beginning to come into being; they are what was called at
the time *Raznochintsy*, the class of educated commoners who, in
a country without a Parliament and lacking political parties,
were excluded from all participation in political life. Moreover,
they found it difficult to make ends meet in an agrarian state in the
hands of feudal landowners, where industrial progress was slight.

At the end of the last century, after the barren vogue of bomb-throwing Anarchism, the *Raznochintsy* found an opening in the Socialist Workers' Movement: 'The right and opportunity of achieving political influence not through the Tzarist bureaucracy of nobles, but through popular representation, and the opportunity of attaining commanding positions in the economy without having a private income.'[3]

Even Vera Zasulich had given up bomb outrages when she briefly returned to Russia in 1900. Lenin himself had long since made up his mind about terrorism. In 1899 he wrote: 'Let us say here and now that, in our personal opinion, terrorism is at present an inefficient means of warfare, and that the Party as a Party must decline to use it until conditions change. . . .'

And two years later, already an émigré in Western Europe, he returned to the subject: 'Basically we have never rejected terrorism, and we cannot reject it. It is a method of warfare which may certainly be used and may even be essential at a definite stage in the battle. But the fact of the matter is that at present . . . such a method of warfare is untimely and inefficient. . . .'

He did not reject the use of Terror, as he himself openly stated again and again; he merely regarded it as 'inefficient at present'. He did not reject it as long as he lived. He used it, and to an unprecedented extent, as soon as he thought it expedient to do so, as was the case in 1917. And he continued to praise Terror from a theoretical point of view after he had become the ruler of the Bolshevist State as openly as he did in 1900. In 1922 he threatened the disaffected in the country with the words:

> You challenged us to battle in its most embittered form in October, and in reply we called forth Terror and the triple Terror. Should it prove necessary again, we will call it forth once more if you make another attempt. Not one worker, not one peasant doubts that it is needed. Nobody doubts it, except hysterical members of the intelligentsia.

A question arises: if Lenin rejected bomb outrages and revolver shots as 'inexpedient', and Terror as generally untimely in 1900, what Terror did he have in mind and under what circumstances did he regard it as expedient?

Terror has been used as an instrument of policy throughout history. It is first the use of violence to achieve political or economic aims; it is the continued use of violence to consolidate these aims when they have been achieved; and, lastly, it is the spreading of fear in order to intimidate potential opponents.

Mankind has displayed a fertile imagination in this field from the start. The extermination of entire tribes and nations was already the practice of victors in Biblical times. In Rome Sulla ordered the compilation of lists of his enemies for unrestricted slaughter. Robespierre's reign of horror at the high tide of the French Revolution was an attempt at Class Terror, the annihilation of an entire social layer considered hostile to the State. And finally the racial Terror of National Socialism consisted of the liquidation of a type of human being regarded as harmful to the community. Yet no system except Lenin's Bolshevism and its further development by Stalin has from the very start made Terror in all its aspects the common basis of power. All other political systems have made at least some pretence at finding faults in their victims, so as to provide some moral justification for the use of Terror. Bolshevism alone has raised Terror to the status of an institution, and made violence a legitimate substitution for law. Dzerzhinsky, the first Head of the Cheka, proclaimed as early as October 1917 in his inaugural proclamation to the Extra-Ordinary Commission for the Suppression of the Counter-Revolution: 'Do not imagine that I have any concern with formal law. We need no justice now. What we need is a fight to the bone. I order, I demand the forging of the revolutionary sword which shall destroy all counter-revolutionaries.'[4]

The Extra-Ordinary Commission for the Suppression of the Counter-Revolution, better known as the Cheka, remained an institution of the Soviet State long after counter-revolutionaries had ceased to exist; from the Cheka it turned into the GPU and then into the NKVD and exists to this day in the form of the KGB. The extermination of all counter-revolutionaries demanded by Dzerzhinsky turned into the extermination of those groups of the population which might at some future date conceivably become potential counter-revolutionaries. No pretence was made of searching out individual guilt: the extermination, for instance, of millions of peasants in the course of the liquidation of the Kulaks showed that membership of a given social stratum was equivalent to a death sentence, if the existence of this stratum was considered 'unhelpful'. This extension of Terror was entirely due to the fact that Bolshevism, as opposed to all other dictatorial systems (including even National Socialism), had incorporated Terror as a political instrument into its ideology openly and from the very start.

The whole development can be traced back to the concept of 'The Dictatorship of the Proletariat', the conviction that one part of mankind has the right to force its will upon the rest of the world. The idea of the Dictatorship of the Proletariat first makes its appearance in a series of articles which Karl Marx wrote in 1850 for the *Neue Rheinische Zeitung*. This series of articles, *The Class Struggles in France*, was written under the impact of the Revolution of 1848 – a Revolution which in the author's opinion had failed. The revolt of the masses had indeed swept away the French monarchy, but in the later stages the bourgeoisie had overthrown the proletariat and set up a parliamentary bourgeois republic. Marx drew from this the following lesson for the future:

> ... The proletariat groups itself more and more round revolutionary socialism, round communism. . . . This socialism is the declaration of the permanent revolution, and of the class dictatorship of the proletariat as a necessary point of transition to the total abolition of class differences, to the abolition of all the relations in production upon which they are founded. . . .

Lenin first encountered Marx when his elder brother Alexander gave him some of Marx's writings. In 1888 he came into contact for the first time with a Marxist Student Circle in Kazan and began to make a thorough study of *Das Kapital*. This study, however, did not lead him to an unquestioning acceptance of the theory. He disregarded the crucial point of Marx's teaching – that dictatorship of the proletariat over other classes could only be established when the masses, impoverished as a result of growing industrialisation, came to represent the majority of the population.

Lenin, on the other hand, forced his will on the majority as the representative of a minority at every decisive moment in his career. Later, in Stalinist practice, the dictatorship no longer represented a transitional stage. Force and Terror remained the means whereby the minority maintained its rule over the majority.

When Lenin founded *Iskra* he already planned to use the periodical to serve his aim – the mobilisation of his own army of professional revolutionaries who would carry the minority to power.

Lenin founded . . . Lenin acted . . . Lenin wrote . . . Lenin said . . . Lenin thought. . . .

Today all Communist writing is permeated with the idea that everything that happened was the work of Lenin. His genius worked out the pattern and it was he who successfully spread it abroad; he asserted his ideas against the opposition of all doubters, opportunists and revisionists, and it is he who shaped the glorious reality of Soviet Russia out of these ideas. Sober facts tell a different story.

'Iskra', the Spark, was the name of a small but very active group of Russian Marxists. Lenin was only one of the three representatives of the group who set out for Switzerland to form a common front with the representatives of the Marxist exiles, Plekhanov, Axelrod and Vera Zasulich. The other two representatives were Alexander Potresov and Julius Martov. Lenin and Potresov were doctrinaire Marxists. Martov had a 'nationalist' slant. He was a Jew; his real name was Yuri Osipovich Zederbaum and he was regarded as the representative of the Bundists, an association founded in 1897, under the title of 'General Jewish Workers in Lithuania, Poland and Russia'. This was probably the best organised of the underground movements, if only because it was easier to unite the Jewish artisans from the small workshops in the ghettos than to organise the proletarians living in large industrial centres under the watchful eye of the secret police. One should not think of these underground organisations as constituting a mass movement in whose ranks marched a million proletarians, or even tens of thousands of well-organised industrial workers. The Russian underground came to life only occasionally when sporadic strikes, disturbances among the peasants or student demonstrations afforded an opportunity for action. The police would then intervene and the spontaneously founded fighting groups would disintegrate again.

The very first of such groups, the South Russian Workers' League, founded in 1875, achieved two hundred members before the police disbanded it. Lenin himself organised with Martov, Potresov and several other intellectuals the 'Petersburg Fighting Union for the Liberation of the Working Class' in the autumn of 1895. By December the circle had already been betrayed by one of its members, a police informer, and was scattered. Lenin and most of his friends found their way to prison and then to Siberia. Next, an attempt was made in March 1898 to weld the conspiratorial circles of the various towns into a single party. In Minsk, nine delegates, representing six organisations, founded the Social Democratic Workers' Party of Russia and decided on the publication of *Rabochaya Gazeta* as the organ of the Party. The Party members were arrested immediately after the Conference and the press intended for the newspaper was confiscated. The whole Social Democratic Workers' Party of Russia numbered only 8,400 members in 1905. Even the Bundists, the strongest of the organisations, had only 23,000 members at that time.

In the large towns the underground was split into individual circles and communication between them was tenuous. One or two issues of illegal newspapers would appear until the police ferreted out the presses. The émigré press reached Russia irregularly and by clandestine means. Even when it successfully evaded the censorship, copies had to be made, duplicated and disseminated at the cost of great trouble and risk. These periodicals waged embittered warfare among themselves, for or against the various shades of socialism – doctrinaire Marxists against revisionist Communists, and both together against 'Narodniki', the despised Populists, who would have nothing to do with industrialisation and the industrial proletariat, and wished to transform Russia into a Socialist Peasant State, without bothering about capitalism. The political leanings of these short-lived publications sometimes changed from number to number, depending upon who had managed to lay hands on the printing presses after the Secret Police had despatched the preceding editorial staff to Siberia. Lenin, for instance, had to see *Rabochee Delo*, the paper of his own Petersburg Fighting Union, reappear as the organ of the Economists against whom he was fighting tooth and nail.

These feuds were no more than wrangles among a handful of theoreticians. Most of them had been living abroad for years, deprived of real contact with the masses whose spokesmen they claimed to be. It is almost touching, for example, to read in Trotsky's Memoirs about the seventeen-year-old student wandering through the streets of the little town of Nikolaev in Southern

Russia until he managed to strike up a conversation with a worker, a genuine proletarian who could tell him what made the workers tick. Trotsky goes on to tell how, having discovered a genuine worker and through him made the acquaintance of a few others, he founded a new South Russian Workers' Union on the spot. In so doing he generously overlooked the fact that his first members belonged to a sect of Bible Students.

These activities at the turn of the century were hardly as yet 'the struggle for the liberation of labour'; they were merely a sort of wordy partisan warfare between ideologists about what could be done and when. The only man who found a way was Lenin. He conceived the plan of organising a cadre of professional revolutionaries within the distributive system of a paper that appeared regularly, held an inflexible line and drove straight for the conquest of power by violence. This was what *Iskra* was intended to be – The Spark that was to kindle the Flame.

The International Workers' Movement had reached a turning-point in its development at about the time when Lenin and *Iskra* entered world history. In 1899 the German Socialist Eduard Bernstein had published *The Assumptions of Socialism and the Tasks of Social Democracy*. The book had the effect of a bomb in Marxist circles. Bernstein had formulated in a sound and scientific way the long-standing doubts of many orthodox Marxists concerning the growing impoverishment of the proletariat and the impending collapse of capitalism, which Marx had so confidently forecast.

There were no signs of this anywhere. Capitalism was entering on mass production to satisfy the consumers of the industrial age. The lot of the proletarians was improving, steadily if not quickly. In Germany, the homeland of the Workers' Movement, Bismarck's social legislation had provided the working man with a minimum of social security since the end of the eighties. Even Tzarist Russia, the most retrograde country in Europe, promulgated a Factory Law in 1882 which limited working hours to eleven and a half a day and forbade the employment of children under twelve. Developments such as these, even among the appalling poverty that still prevailed, indicated that some day capitalism itself would acquire an interest in the prosperity of the working class, since it comprised the future customers for the mass products of industry.

Bernstein's new doctrine was labelled 'revisionism'. It refused to engage in a revolution aimed at liquidating the bourgeois state and sought instead to direct social democracy into parliamentary channels in order to win political equality, material security and, ultimately, prosperity for the proletariat.

European Socialism and Social Democracy in its various forms have been revisionist ever since, sometimes against the wishes of the leadership in individual countries. Karl Kautsky, the great theoretician of German socialism, spent much of his life refuting Lenin's accusations that he was a revisionist, an opportunist and a liquidator of Marxism. He wrote: 'The aim of our political struggle remains constant: the conquest of power in the state through Parliament, and the elevation of Parliament to authority over the Government.'

The ruthless passion displayed by Lenin in fighting those who contradicted him showed for the first time in his dispute with the Economist Bahn. The success of revisionism in Russia at the turn of the century was a result of special circumstances there. The two and a half million factory workers represented hardly ten per cent of the population. No revolution could be mounted with such a small proportion of proletarians and, certainly, no dictatorship of the proletariat could be set up. Since there was no Parliament, the struggle for workers' rights could not even be brought into party politics. There was nothing left for the Economists, as the Russian revisionists were called, except a purely industrial struggle. Trade Unionism, as they saw it, was the only road.

Lenin was to show that they were wrong. He achieved a revolution with an infinitesimally small minority. And he succeeded in setting up a dictatorship. In 1900 his motto had been: 'He who dominates the Central Organisation dominates the Party Congress. He who dominates the Party Congress dominates the Party.'

By October 1917 this had become: 'He who dominates the Petersburg Soviet of Workers' and Soldiers' Deputies, dominates the capital. He who dominates the capital, dominates Russia.' The Economists were proved wrong because Lenin based himself on an ideology of violence and did not renounce Terror as a system. Yet he also had no intention of applying the Marxist recipe to Russia without modification. He did not want to wait until the proletariat was 'ripe' to seize power. But he did not diverge from Marx as the Economists did – he went beyond Marx.

His solution was the seizure of power by a minority using violence as its instrument. In order to use violence effectively against the majority, which in effect meant a whole nation, an organisation of practitioners of violence was needed. These could only be professional revolutionaries from whom Lenin demanded that they should devote to the Revolution 'not only their free evenings, but their entire lives' and *Iskra* was to be the means of mobilising them. Lenin was quite open about this. He stated his intention clearly:

> A permanent organisation will come into being wholly of its own accord, through the paper and in connection with it. . . . The technical problem alone, the need to supply the paper regularly with material and to arrange for its regular distribution, will demand the creation of a network of trusted members of the unified Party . . . who will try out their talents in the organisation of one revolutionary act or another. . . . Such a degree of readiness for action can only be achieved through the unrelenting activity of regular troops.

Lenin was quite clear in his own mind that the revolution could not start from the peasantry, spread out as it was over the whole of this immeasurably vast land. It could only come from the industrial proletariat concentrated in the great towns. He realised equally clearly that the proletarian masses were only capable of sporadic action, unless they submitted to a well-organised leadership. Such a leadership in turn must itself receive orders from a central General Staff. This military structure arose from the operational need to seize power at a word of command, since the revolution was conceived from the very start as a revolution by a minority. It was not the masses who would sweep away a tyrannical upper class in order to take over the State intact; a handful of theoreticians would arrogate power to themselves over the heads of millions in order to construct the ideal State.

It is clear that in reality the proletariat wished only for a chance to rise to the lower middle class. Similarly the peasants longed not for agrarian socialism, but merely for the ownership of land. Communism would grant neither of these wishes: its entire intellectual edifice rested on the fervent conviction of the founders that they alone had discovered the right way to Heaven on Earth. This conviction appeared incontrovertible to them, irrefutable because it had been worked out scientifically. Those for whom this paradise was intended would first have to be educated against their will.

Given this creed, the rules of power followed automatically. First, dictatorship of the proletariat over the other classes of the population; then dictatorship of the Party officials over the proletariat; lastly, dictatorship of the Party leadership over the Party officials; to crown the edifice, dictatorship of the Head of the Party over the Party leadership. Only Mass Terror could keep this mechanism going, in terms of Marxist, then Leninist and finally Stalinist practice. Marx had proclaimed the dictatorial takeover of power as a transitional measure when fully developed capitalism collapsed. Lenin's party of professional revolutionaries took dictatorial powers in order to overthrow a capitalism which was not in the least developed, and to build a classless society before the time was ripe. During the 'period of education', the professional revolutionaries had to maintain themselves in power through Terror because the promised new classless society in the paradise of workers and peasants could only be created, if at all, by degrees and at the cost of unprecedented sacrifices.

It became apparent during the Stalin era that new classes were taking the place of those that had been liquidated. The Party bureaucrats who had risen to the position of a new feudal class rebelled against the top leadership of the Party. The Party leadership was forced to hold on to power by means of Terror; and this was the crucial element of Stalinism at the height of the waves of purges.

The latest stage of Soviet development is the rise of the technocrats.

Stalin's heirs had to decide, when they themselves were by no means secure, whether this pressure could be held back by renewed Terror. The post-Stalin leadership, placed in this dilemma by economic progress, and doubtless influenced by the situation abroad, finally decided to relinquish power piecemeal, so as to be able to do away with the Terror step by step.

SOURCES

1. Article 4 of the Fundamental Law of the Russian Empire.

2. James Joll, *The Anarchists* (Little, Brown and Company, Boston, 1965).

3. Hermann F. Achminow, *Die Totengraeber des Kommunismus* (Stuttgart, 1964).

4. Georg von Rauch, *History of Soviet Russia* (Frederick A. Praeger, New York, 1964).

CHAPTER TWO

The Dress Rehearsal

In the summer of 1903, the Okhrana, the Tzarist Secret Police, put its organisation abroad into high gear. A sudden travel fever seemed to have seized various people on whom the Okhrana had long since had its eye. Then Dr. Jakob Zhitomirski provided the requisite evidence: the Social Democratic Workers' Party of Russia intended to hold its Second Party Conference in Brussels.

Dr. Zhitomirski knew the facts if anyone did. He was a member of the Organisation Committee; his fellow organisers, of course, did not know that by his real profession he was an Okhrana agent. He enjoyed Lenin's special confidence. On every matter in dispute he unhesitatingly voted with Lenin – naturally enough, since his main assignment was to keep tabs on Lenin and report every detail about him to Petersburg.

Lenin may have been surprised that he was set free so quickly in 1900 when he fell into the hands of the Okhrana during his illegal stay in Leningrad, and that neither his passport nor the money intended for *Iskra* should have been confiscated. The Okhrana knew exactly what it was doing. Neither the dispute between the Economists and the doctrinaire Marxists, nor the passion with which Lenin fought the Economists had escaped the attention of the Tzarist Secret Police. From its point of view, however, the Economists with their trade union ambitions were by far the most dangerous enemies; nobody thought much of the handful of Marxist ideologists and their dreams about the dictatorship of the proletariat.

So it was that Lenin went free. He was thereby removed from Russia where he had been in direct contact with the workers, and it was hoped that the doctrinaire single-mindedness of the man would successfully cause a split among the émigrés. Many years later, in the spring of 1917, the German High Command allowed the Russian émigré Lenin to travel through Germany to a Russia already shaken by the first tremors of the Revolution but still at war; Winston Churchill later compared the sealed train in which Lenin travelled to a test tube carrying a plague bacillus. The Okhrana had already applied this principle in 1900. It would seem, however, that the significance of Lenin's staff work in building up a private army of professional revolutionaries never became clear to the authorities. Indeed, if Lenin had been better known at that time, his plans would have struck his contemporaries as something out of a political science-fiction story.

Lenin, the organiser of violence and Terror from his shabby lodging, a pen his only weapon, wrote, talked, discussed, complained, swore and cursed, and wrote again. He prepared and worked out the theory of the seizure of power by an underground movement – a movement which consisted at first of himself alone – and power over a world empire that stretched from the edge of central Europe to the Pacific Ocean. Who could really have believed at the beginning of this century that this fiction would one day become sober truth?

Small wonder then that the Okhrana also regarded Lenin, for the time being at any rate, as by far the less dangerous opponent. Indeed the entire Second Party Conference of Russian Social Democracy also looked anything but dangerous when it began in Brussels on 30th July 1903.

The neighbourhood of the highly respectable 'Coq d'Or' restaurant provided the setting for the grotesque spectacle of what turned out to be Dostoevsky's 'Demons' played as pantomime. A couple of dozen weird, often rather shabby figures emerged from stuffy lodgings all over Western Europe into the broad daylight of the elegant Belgian capital. The conference developed amid the hysteria typical of émigré gatherings accompanied by the deafening racket of an open-air meeting. The innocent neighbours were woken from their sleep. An émigré named Koltsov, who lived in a rented room close to the 'Coq d'Or', acted as the reception committee; his landlord, however, soon made it clear that he would get notice to quit without delay if any more sinister foreigners came ringing at the door. So Koltsov and his wife had to take turns at the front door to greet the delegates with passionate embraces and loud kisses on the cheek in true Russian style, and to launch the first stormy discussions about the impending collapse of capitalism even before they were in the house.

The first act of the fall of the Russian empire was played out as a tragi-comedy under the eyes of the agents of the Okhrana. Any more or less experienced agent would have come to the conclusion that Imperial rule stood in little danger from these voluble coffee-house intellectuals who tore each other to pieces in the endless procedural debates. He would have been wrong, but only because of the presence of Lenin.

It is important to have a clear picture of the Utopian helplessness displayed by the delegates to the Second Party Conference of the Social Democratic Workers' Party of Russia in the summer of 1903 in order to assess Lenin correctly at this early stage in his career. He himself did not think much of the meeting and soon found an unflattering description for the mass of the delegates – 'The Bog'. These were certainly not the professional revolutionaries who would establish dictatorship over the proletariat. Lenin fought his way through the Party Conference merely because it could give him the legitimate authority he needed to speak, not merely as an individual, but in the name of a Party.

The very organisation of the Brussels meeting was complicated and confusing. There were fifty-one votes and fifty-two participants. But of these only forty-two could vote, while nine had two votes each because they represented larger groups. Ten delegates were there only in a consultative capacity. This system had been arranged by an organisational committee largely under Lenin's guidance. The delegates from within Russia were intended to provide a representative cross-section of the individual illegal workers' circles in the industrial areas. As soon, however, as the delegates had been chosen a wave of arrests sent those elected to prison; the substitutes came chiefly from the new 'Iskra' agencies. Indeed, the whole system of selection involved a double deception: delegates of the 'Iskra' group were to give the impression to the remainder, who were mostly émigrés, that they had behind them a powerful Russian underground movement, a movement to be reckoned with; at the same time, workers' circles in Russia were to be made to feel that the Party Conference in Brussels represented a powerful, unified Party whose instructions must be obeyed.

It is true that by 1903 *Iskra* already had some authority among the Russian proletariat. Lenin's plan to build a network of agents by means of the distributing organisation of the paper was bearing fruit. Since 1900 no less than forty-five numbers of *Iskra* had appeared fairly regularly, which was more than any other periodical of this kind had succeeded in doing, either abroad or within Russia itself. Even though only part of each edition reached its destination – Northern Russia via Stockholm, and the Caucasian oilfields by way of Marseilles – this was an improvement on any earlier effort, and illegal presses within Russia ensured that further copies were available.

One such illegal press was set up in Baku and it is here that Stalin makes his first appearance.

Iskra was providing the Russian workers' circles with information and ideological instruction, and it bore the imprint of Lenin's personality. When the three promoters of *Iskra*, Lenin, Martov and Potresov, went to Switzerland in 1900, they concluded a regular agreement with Plekhanov, Axelrod and Vera Zasulich to ensure that all the editors had equal rights. Every article was to be approved by all the editors. Lenin, however, immediately began to squeeze out the older editors. At his suggestion, production of the periodical was transferred to Germany, far from Geneva. This gave Lenin a good deal of independence, even though articles now had to be sent back and forth by post among the six editors. He also arranged that his wife, Nadezhda Krupskaya, should become the editorial secretary, so that he could supervise all correspondence. The laxity, not to say laziness, of some of his colleagues helped him. When the work done for *Iskra* was analysed at the Party Conference in Brussels, it emerged that Plekhanov had contributed twenty-four articles, Potresov eight, Vera Zasulich six, the often ailing Axelrod only four, while Lenin had written a total of thirty-two. Only Martov had been busier than Lenin: he had contributed thirty-nine articles. And although Martov officially came to Brussels as a representative from *Iskra*, he retained his Jewish allegiance and remained close to the Bund, the Jewish Workers' League, still the largest single organisation in the Russian underground.

The earlier émigrés had nicknamed Lenin and Martov 'The Twins' when they had first come from Russia. Three years later, on the eve of the Party Conference, they had already been embittered opponents for some time. They had split over the draft of the Party programme on which the Party Conference was to vote, and the Conference turned into a duel between the two men. Martov suggested the following wording for Paragraph 1 of the Party Programme – 'Anyone will be regarded as a member of the Social Democratic Workers' Party of Russia who acknowledges its Programme and supports the Party both from a material point of view and by work under the supervision and leadership of one of the Party organisations.' Lenin's draft appeared to be very similar: 'Anyone will be regarded as a member of the Social Democratic Workers' Party of Russia who acknowledges its Programme and supports the Party, both from a material point of view and by personal participation in one of the Party organisations.'

One must read the two drafts more than once before spotting the fine distinction between them. The delegates, however, well drilled in ideological finesse, saw the point immediately. It was simply the old dispute as to whether the Party should include the masses of the proletariat, or only an élite of activists. 'Under the supervision and leadership of the Party', or 'In the Party' dealt with the question of whether the Party should support every movement and trend provided it worked for the proletariat, or whether the promoters of individual movements and trends should submit to the Party leadership if they wished to stay in the Party. In other words, the point at issue was whether the proletariat stood above the Party or the Party above the proletariat.

Lenin had been at pains to ensure that the fundamental difference underlying the words should be crystal clear to the delegates. Most of the pundits of the Workers' Movement had read his pamphlet 'What is to be done?' published a year earlier. In it one could read sentences such as the following which appear throughout the two hundred pages of this manual on the seizure of power:

> Strict conspiratorial activity is impossible if the organisation has a broad membership. . . .
> . . . The Social Democrat must think first and foremost about an organisation of revolutionaries.
> . . . Everything that needs to be done will be done by this organisation without members.

Lenin's comprehensive recipe for revolution meant placing the proletariat under tutelage. He quite simply denied it the capacity of helping itself, and demanded a 'Drive from outside' through a 'Committee of professional revolutionaries'. He demanded that 'only those members should participate in the organisation who engage professionally in revolutionary activities and are professionally trained in the art of fighting the political police'. Lenin's conclusion was: 'Give us an organisation of revolutionaries and we will lift Russia from its hinges.'

Russia was indeed lifted from its hinges fourteen years later, as was a sizeable part of the globe in the decades that followed. For the delegates who met in Brussels in the summer of 1903, such a vision of the future amounted to a nightmare. They saw in it not the dictatorship of the proletariat but, on the contrary, dictatorship over the proletariat, the rule of a small élite of violent men over the rest of mankind. At the vote, there was a parting of minds: Martov's draft secured twenty-eight votes, while Lenin's text obtained only twenty-three. Not even Lenin's own 'Iskra' organisation had stood fast behind its leader. What happened next foreshadowed the use of Terror by the Party leadership against the Party officials. The members of the 'Iskra' group were summoned to a series of secret meetings in order to restore unanimity. Martov and his supporters were to be brought back to the pre-arranged 'General Line'.

In the course of these consultations, a secret Party Conference within the Party Conference itself, Martov's group was outvoted on a series of resolutions. And Lenin demanded assurances from all its members that they would obey group discipline and would vote in open session with the majority of the 'Iskra' group, against their own convictions.

However slight the significance of this event may seem today, its importance in the analysis of the whole concept of 'Communist Democracy' is very great. It was the first example of how things were to be fixed, and have been fixed again and again throughout the Lenin, Stalin and Khrushchev eras, whenever it has been a matter of converting a minority into a majority by manipulation, and then brutally suppressing all opposition on the strength of this dubious 'majority'. The system works according to the precept: 'Divide the Party and rule it.' Given even the slenderest majority among the top leadership, it forces those voting against a motion to vote obediently in favour of it in the next widest forum, in the name of discipline. Thus, step by step, an agreement is achieved which, in the final analysis, is nothing more than the acceptance of the orders of a few men at the top, or even those of a single individual. The next stage followed logically: anyone contradicting the supposed agreement became an 'Enemy of the Party', and as soon as the Party had achieved power, the sequel was obvious: Enemies of the Party must be liquidated! There was as yet no question in 1903 of physical liquidation. All that could be done was to ease them out. The first to be eased out were the Bundists.

The five delegates who represented the Bund, the Jewish Workers' League, had come to Brussels with a very definite set of demands. They required autonomy for the League in all matters pertaining to the Jewish proletariat. Fear of violence haunted Russian Jews, and more particularly so during the previous two decades. The average Russian is inclined to be anti-semitic; since the assassination of Tzar Alexander II, in which a Jewish girl student had taken a leading part, this latent anti-semitism had found an outlet in a wave of pogroms. The pogroms took place chiefly in the small peasant townships, but Jewish workers did not feel at ease even among proletarians. Moreover, they were usually well-trained craftsmen, more intelligent and therefore better paid than their non-Jewish fellow workers. They were afraid that traditional anti-semitism and their relatively higher standard of living might make them the first victims in a revolution.

To make matters worse, the Bundists themselves were competing with the emergent Zionists. They had to make room in their programme for the awakening of national consciousness among Jews and, for instance, to place a strong emphasis on the value of the Yiddish language if they were to avoid losing support. Such a programme, however, could only provoke Lenin's embittered enmity. He planned a unitary, tightly organised, conspiratorial Party, not a loose association that allowed for national autonomy. Most of the Party members were at one with him in this. And so the demands of the Bundists were voted down by a majority of the delegates, including the Jewish members of the 'Iskra' group, Axelrod, Martov and Leo Deutsch.

This interlude is worth noting. It foreshadows one direction which the Terror was later to take, that of anti-semitism. This might be baffling, given a Party so richly endowed with Jewish intellectuals. The comments of the editor of Lenin's

Collected Works about the Bundists at the Party Conference of
1903 are enlightening:

> Although it formally belonged to the Social Democratic Workers'
> Party of Russia, the Bund was a bourgeois-nationalistic organisation
> by nature. . . . The Bund dissolved itself in March 1921 and a part of
> its membership joined the Communist Party of Russia (Bolsheviks)
> as individuals after satisfying the normal requirements. There were
> some double-dealers among these Bundists who joined the Party in
> order to undermine it from within; they were later uncovered as
> enemies of the people.

Even though Stalin's racial Terror fell infinitely short of the
National-Socialist 'Final Solution', it was virulent enough, as
we shall see. It was in evidence in the notorious concentration
camp area of the Karaganda mining district where the majority
of émigré German and Austrian socialists were interned. It
played a role after 1945 in the People's Democracies, for instance
in the Slansky trial in Czechoslovakia and its aftermath. And only
Stalin's death prevented an even more dreadful outcome for the
last large-scale purge of the Stalin era, the so-called Doctors'
Plot, with its anti-semitic slant.

It may appear puzzling in this context that for so many years
Stalin should have entrusted the direction of the GPU – the prop
of his reign of Terror – to Yagoda, a Jew. But it is part of the
technique of Terror to put an outsider in charge of the organisation which operates it, a member of a despised, even hated minority
who has been made to feel the distaste of the society which
surrounds him, and dislikes it equally in his turn. Dzerzhinsky,
Lenin's first Head of the Cheka, was a Pole, and the hatred of
Poles for Russians is proverbial. Then came a Jew, Yagoda, to
head an organisation designed to subjugate a traditionally
anti-semitic population. The last of the series was Lavrenti
Beria, the Georgian, and nowhere in the Soviet Union is
nationalist feeling stronger than in the Caucasus.

As a result of their defeat the Bundists left the Party Conference
in 1903. The Martov group thereby lost five important votes.
Lenin then launched his second attack, over the recognition of
Iskra as the sole organ of the émigré groups. The periodical
Rabochee Delo, founded by Lenin himself in Petersburg, had
now fallen into the hands of the Economists and was to be

abolished. On this point Lenin secured a majority. The *Rabochee Delo* question proved crucial for him: both delegates of the group that edited the periodical followed the Bundists and withdrew from the Conference. Vladimir Ilyich Ulyanov, who had left Russia only three years earlier as an insignificant émigré, now commanded a majority of two at the Conference of the Social Democratic Workers' Party.

By these two votes he made world history. He called his group 'Bolsheviki', which meant in Russian the members of a majority. He could run down all those contradicting him as 'Mensheviki', or representatives of a minority. When those who had been outsmarted realised what had happened it was too late. The label of Mensheviki remained with them even into the decisive days of 1917. They were not clever enough to shake it off: the double deception had succeeded. Lenin, the Bolshevik, could now claim that he represented the Party, and he hammered this lesson home tirelessly into the Russian proletariat, carefully disregarding the fact that the true majority was not with the Party leadership. The fate of the majority was easy enough to forecast once the minority group which had manipulated itself into a controlling position secured effective power to subjugate opponents, and then to liquidate them. This is what gives the Party Conference of 1903 its importance. It was the successful dress rehearsal for the Great Terror to come.

The Revolution was barely six weeks old when Lenin returned to Russia from exile in Switzerland on 3rd April 1917. It had followed the pattern of the French Revolution of 1848 which had caused Marx to call for the dictatorship of the proletariat. Tzarism had been swept away by food strikes, working class demonstrations against the war and a mutiny of the Petrograd garrison. Power, however, had gone to the conservative middle-class majority in the Duma and not to the workers. On 27th February the mutinous troops had already been in control of the capital for some time but the Duma was still casting about helplessly for some way of establishing a government. It was then that Shulgin, a Conservative Representative, exclaimed: 'If we do not seize power, others will do so – those who have already elected some scoundrels in the factories.'

The 'scoundrels' referred to by Shulgin were in session in

Room 13 of the Tauride Palace, put at the disposal of the Petrograd Soviet of the Workers' and Soldiers' Deputies by the President of the Duma. (The word 'soviet' means 'council' in Russian, and originally applied to the committees which sprang up more or less spontaneously in Russian factories during the revolution of 1905. After 1917 it gradually came to apply to the Bolshevik régime as a whole.) This particular Soviet undoubtedly dominated the streets, factories and barracks of Petrograd but, strangely enough, it made not the slightest attempt to take over the Government. It did not even allow its members to enter the Provisional Government then being formed under Prince Lvov, except for a lawyer, Alexander Kerensky, a left-wing Labour Group Representative who was also one of the two Deputy Chairmen of the Executive Committee of the Soviet. Kerensky became Minister of Justice, and thus a kind of Soviet ambassador and observer in the Government.

The Petrograd Soviet was formed in the first days of the Revolution on the pattern of the Workers' Councils of 1905. It consisted of some two hundred and fifty delegates elected somewhat hastily and informally in the barracks and factories. The Duma Representative Nicholas Chkheidze had been elected Chairman. The other Deputy Chairman was also a Duma Representative, the Menshevik Matvei Skobelev who had at one time shared Trotsky's exile. The political complexion of the leadership of the Executive Committee is in itself an indication of the slight importance attached by the workers and soldiers to the Bolsheviks during the early period of the Revolution. Lenin's Party only succeeded in carrying a Bolshevik resolution in the Petrograd Soviet and achieving a majority in a properly run election in Moscow six months later.

Nevertheless, when Lenin arrived at the Finland station he was solemnly met by Chkheidze on behalf of the Petrograd Soviet and cheered by a vast crowd. This welcome however was addressed to the indomitable revolutionary whose name was familiar to the industrial proletariat from hundreds of articles, handouts, proclamations and pamphlets rather than to the Party leader.

In so far as the masses were concerned, the difference between Mensheviks and Bolsheviks was slight, and most Mensheviks still regarded Lenin and his followers as a left-wing group in the

Party with which a joint policy would have to be agreed sooner or later.

A number of attempts to re-unify the Party had failed since the great split of 1903. Although they called themselves Bolsheviks, Lenin's committees had always formed a minority in the Social Democratic Workers' Party of Russia. The two groups did achieve a common platform during the elections to the Fourth Duma, when the Mensheviks won seven seats in Parliament while the Bolsheviks secured six. The Bolsheviks were unlucky in the Duma. One of their representatives, Roman Malinovski, secretly a police spy, was ordered by the Okhrana to resign his seat, while the remaining five Bolshevik representatives were arrested soon after the outbreak of war. This left the Mensheviks as the only representatives of Social Democracy in the Duma.

In fact, the Social Democrats were united only in name, and only insofar as the Mensheviks were concerned. After nine years of unsuccessful efforts either to win over the Mensheviks or to out-vote them, Lenin called a conference of the Bolshevik group in Prague in 1912 which resulted in the foundation of a new Party. Soviet official history describes the event as follows:

> The Prague Conference drew up the balance of the entire struggle of the Bolsheviks against opportunism and resolved to exclude the Mensheviks from the Party. After the exclusion of the Mensheviks the Prague Conference formed the Bolshevik Party as a party existing independently. By bringing to an end the ideological and organisational bankruptcy of the Mensheviks and driving them out of the Party the Bolsheviks took over the old banner of the Party, the Social Democratic Workers' Party of Russia. It is for this reason that the Party of the Bolsheviks continued to call itself until 1918 the Social Democratic Workers' Party of Russia with the addition of the word 'Bolsheviks' in brackets.[1]

This highly slanted account of events conceals the fact that the Bolsheviks could not get the better of the Menshevik majority and were forced to found a party of their own, but continued to make use of the old label with an inconspicuous addition. According to Bolshevik information the new party had about ten thousand members at the start. The fact that this tiny splinter group achieved power in Russia five years later is due solely to Lenin. His plan for the mobilisation of an army of professional revolutionaries had stood the test of action. It might have failed but for the unrelenting passion and extraordinary energy with which Lenin put his plans into force. In 1910, at the Stockholm Conference, when the struggle between Mensheviks and Bolsheviks was agitating the entire Socialist International, somebody asked the veteran revolutionary Axelrod: 'Are you suggesting that all these splits, quarrels and rows are the work of a single man? How is it that one man can be at once so successful and so dangerous?' Axelrod replied: 'There is no other man in the whole world who is so wrapped up in revolution for twenty-four hours a day, who has no other thought but that of revolution and who even when he is asleep dreams of nothing but revolution. You try it – how could anyone get the better of such a man?'[2] In spite of this the non-Bolshevik majority of the Petrograd Soviet still believed in April 1917 that it could get the better of Lenin. Chkheidze's speech of welcome at the station held a note of warning: 'Comrade Lenin, we welcome you to Russia in the name of the Petrograd Soviet and the entire Revolution, but we believe that the chief task of the revolutionary democracy is to defend our Revolution against all attacks, internal and external. We hope that you will join us in pursuing this aim!'

Lenin had no intention of doing so. His own aim remained seizure of power by the Bolsheviks. It became clearer and clearer during the summer of 1917 that the only way to success was an armed rising.

Lenin had no illusions about the strength of his following. On the very night of his arrival he stated a number of theses at a Bolshevik meeting in the Kshesinsky Palace. They were published in *Pravda* on 7th April under the headlines 'Concerning the task of the proletariat during the current Revolution'. The fourth thesis is perhaps the most notable: 'Recognition of the fact that our Party is in a minority, for the time being even in a weak minority, in relation to the block of all the petit-bourgeois opportunistic elements who are under the influence of the bourgeoisie and are carrying this influence into the proletariat. . . .'

This clear understanding of the situation still did not make Lenin inclined to capitulate. On the contrary, he favoured a demonstrative separation from the majority. His April theses contained the following proposal: 'Instead of adopting the name of Social Democracy, whose official leaders have betrayed Socialism throughout the world by defecting to the bourgeoisie

... we must adopt the name of Communist Party.' It took a year to change the name but Lenin's programme was firm from the day of his arrival – to seize power by means of the Communist minority. As soon as the organisation of professional revolutionaries had seized power by force the masses would obey those in authority.

A few months after the Party split in 1903, the Polish Social Democrat Rosa Luxemburg stated her view of Lenin's plan for a party of professional revolutionaries in a long article published in the *Neue Zeit*. Lenin's low opinion of the moral strength of the proletariat and his suggestion that a small élite of intellectuals should assume organisational control over the working masses disturbed her.

> Nothing so easily and surely delivers a fledgling workers' movement to the lust for power of the theoreticians as restriction within the iron bands of bureaucratic centralism. It degrades the militant workers and makes them pliable instruments of a 'Committee'. Let us not forget that the revolution about to dawn in Russia is a middle-class, not a proletarian revolution ... therefore, the less play is given to independent activity, free initiative, political thinking among the most awakened layer of the working class and the more this layer is politically fettered and drilled by a Social Democrat Central Committee, the more easy the game will be for the middle-class demagogues in the new Russia. And so tomorrow the harvest of today's labours of Social Democracy will find its way all the more readily into the barns of the bourgeoisie.

Rosa Luxemburg was wrong in fearing that the middle class would reap the fruit of Social Democrat labours. Lenin's armed October rising gave the middle class no time to establish itself. But she was right in forecasting that the working class would be degraded into the willing instrument of a 'Committee'.

Late in 1918, when the October Revolution was barely one year old, Rosa Luxemburg, then in prison in Germany, made another forecast about the future consequences of the dictatorship over the proletariat.

> Life dies away in every public institution without general elections, without complete freedom of press and assembly, without free debate. It becomes a pretence at life in which bureaucracy remains the sole active element. Public life gradually goes to sleep. A few dozen tirelessly active party leaders direct and rule. Among them a

dozen outstanding ones are the real leaders and an élite of workers
is summoned to meet from time to time in order to clap the speeches
of the leaders and to vote unanimously for pre-arranged resolutions.
In other words it is, at base, a clique economy, a dictatorship indeed
but not the dictatorship of the proletariat. It is the dictatorship of a
bunch of politicians, a dictatorship in the middle-class sense. . . .
One can go further: such conditions must lead to growing savagery
in public life: assassinations, shooting of hostages, etc. . . .

These words were written in the autumn of 1918, many years
before Stalin's rise to power fulfilled Rosa Luxemburg's forecast
word for word.

A handful of politicians had established themselves in a giant
empire reaching from Eastern Europe to the Pacific Ocean. In
October 1917 however their power did not extend much beyond
the limits of Petrograd and Moscow. A year later the territory
ruled by the Council of People's Commissars had shrunk practically to the limits of the former Grand Duchy of Moscow.
Finland, Belorussia, the Baltic States and the Caucasus had
fallen away and set up national governments. German troops held
the Ukraine. The jurisdiction of the counter-revolutionary
Government in Omsk extended from the Urals to the Pacific.
British, French, American and Japanese troops had intervened
in Murmansk, Archangel, the Turkestan and Vladivostok. In
Southern Russia Denikin's White Army was operating in the
vicinity of Tzaritsyn, later Stalingrad. A regime that wished to
retain power under such circumstances had only one last resort –
Terror.

SOURCES
 1. *History of the Communist Party of the Soviet Union* (Moscow, 1938).
 2. Bertram D. Wolfe, *Three who Made a Revolution* (Dial Press, New
York, 1948).

Part Two

THE FLAME

CHAPTER THREE

The Dictatorship over the Proletariat

O N the evening of 15th August 1943, Iosif Vissarionivich Stalin stood at the sideboard in the dining-room of his four-roomed flat in the Kremlin and with his own hands uncorked a whole battery of bottles. The refreshments were intended for him and the men who sat round the table: Molotov, his Foreign Minister, a Russian Interpreter, the British Major Birse, who also acted as interpreter and Winston Churchill, the British Prime Minister. They were waiting for the draft of the communiqué about the Anglo-Soviet talks of the previous day. A red-headed girl, Stalin's daughter, had laid the table, an old housekeeper had brought the food, and both women had then vanished. Towards midnight, when both the drinking and the conversation were tailing off, Winston Churchill put a direct question to his Russian host: 'Tell me, have the stresses of this war been as bad to you personally as carrying through the policy of the Collective Farms?' 'Oh, no,' replied Stalin, 'the Collective Farm policy was a terrible struggle.' Churchill continued to probe: 'I thought you would have found it bad because you were not dealing with a few score thousands of aristocrats or big landowners but with millions of small men.' Stalin held up both hands with the fingers spread out: 'Ten millions. It was fearful. Four years it lasted. It was absolutely necessary for Russia, if we were to avoid periodic famines, to plough the land with tractors.' Stalin went on talking about the tractors and concluded: 'We took the greatest trouble to explain it to the peasants. It was no use arguing with them. After you have said all you can to a peasant, he says he must go home and consult his wife and his herd.'

Churchill wanted to know details and Stalin finally admitted: 'Many of them agreed to come in with us. Some of them were given land of their own to cultivate in the province of Tomsk or the province of Irkutsk or farther North but the great bulk were very unpopular and were wiped out by their labourers.'

At this point the conversation was interrupted because Cadogan, Churchill's secretary, brought in the draft communiqué. The short conversation had, however, made such an impression on Churchill that he reproduced it many years later in his Memoirs. He added his own thoughts about it:

> I record as they come back to me these memories, and the strong impression I sustained at the moment of millions of men and women being blotted out or displaced for ever. A generation would no doubt come to whom their miseries were unknown, but it would be sure of having more to eat and bless Stalin's name.[1]

Winston Churchill was to be proved wrong. Fourteen years later, at the Twentieth Congress, a generation which could undoubtedly eat better did not bless Stalin's name – it cursed him.

The Terror, whose millions of victims among the peasantry Stalin numbered on his ten fingers, began on the 20th December 1917. It began in the shadow of the light blue and gold domes of a former convent on the edge of the old city of Petersburg, at the point where the Neva bends south. The three-storied building of the Smolny Institute had been an educational establishment for aristocratic young ladies. By the autumn of 1917 the revolutionary storm had long since scattered the former pupils and the door plates of the various classrooms were now painted over with a multiplicity of abbreviations indicating the new occupants. The Smolny Institute had become the headquarters of the Bolsheviks.

Dzerzhinsky had his office in a small corner room at the end of a long passage. His original function was to command the heavily armed guard of the Party Headquarters. Dzerzhinsky was then forty years of age, a native of Vilna in Poland and an engineer by profession. He came from a rich land-owning family. He was a Pole and his hatred for the Tzarist régime which had turned Poland into a conquered province was perhaps the original impulse that had set him on his way. He had joined the Polish Social Democrats, and as chance would have it he was in a Moscow prison when the February Revolution brought down the Tzar in 1917: he attended the first session of the Moscow Soviet, which had just been formed, in his prison clothes. At this time there was as yet no sign of Lenin, then still in Switzerland. However, as early as 1908, Lenin had been in contact with Dzerzhinsky, who together with Trotsky published *Pravda* in Vienna. Lenin decided to bring out the *Proletari* in Vienna as well. Dzerzhinsky served as intermediary between him and Dr. Viktor Adler, the leader of the Austrian Social Democrats. Everything was done quite openly under the glittering chandeliers of the writers' cafés in the plushy surroundings of the old Imperial city. Vienna of the Waltzes regarded the café conspirators as something equally out of an operetta; only the future revolutionaries took themselves seriously.

This was in 1908. Nine years later what had seemed an operetta turned into a blood-soaked melodrama. The former café conspirators ruled over life and death. In due course Dzerzhinsky left Moscow and went to Petersburg where Lenin, the former advocate, Trotsky, the Ukrainian landowner's son and Stalin, the scientific assistant from the Tiflis Observatory, had seized power. It was still a shaky power. These men ruled over Petersburg, re-named Petrograd in 1914, and by a decree of 27th October 1917 they issued the following proclamation: 'The authority of the Government is exercised by the College of Chairman of these Commissions, that is by the Council of People's Commissars.' At the moment all this was more theory than practice. The war was still in progress along the whole of the enormous front stretching from Estonia to the Black Sea. Although the garrisons in Petrograd and Moscow had rallied to the Soviet of Workers, the Council of People's Commissars could only reach the millions of soldiers at the front by the direct telephone line which connected the Seat of Government with G.H.Q. The transcript of a telephone conversation has survived from these strange times. At the G.H.Q. end of the line was the Commander-in-Chief, General Dukhonin, and at the other end, in Petrograd, stood Lenin, Stalin and the new Minister of War Krylenko. It was long past midnight. General Dukhonin heard Lenin saying: 'In the name of the Government of the Russian Republic, and as instructed by the Council of People's Commissars, we relieve you of your appointment. Ensign Krylenko has been appointed Commander-in-Chief.' One can imagine the feelings of the General whom the Council of People's Commissars had fetched from his bed to inform him by telephone that Ensign Krylenko was taking command of the entire Russian Army. To Dukhonin and many others it must have seemed that this absurd pack of plotters would be easy to sweep away.

With a mixture of rage and despair, Lenin cried: 'Can we

really not find among us a Fouquier-Tinville, to tame our wild counter-revolutionaries?'[2] Fouquier-Tinville, Robespierre's public prosecutor, had sent thousands to the guillotine in order to maintain the reign of Terror. What Lenin needed even more was a Joseph Fouché, Napoleon's Chief of Police, a genius to organise a new Bolshevist Okhrana, a merciless head hunter. He needed a man with Fouché's talents, but without his vanity and his love for intrigue, and a Fouquier-Tinville who would be prepared to deliver every victim required, incorruptible and without personal ambition. Only thus could the danger be avoided that such a man would turn the power he had been given against those who had given it to him. Lenin found his mixture of Fouché and Fouquier-Tinville in a small corner room at the end of a long corridor in the Smolny Institute. It was Felix Edmundovich Dzerzhinsky.

The first conflict between contending groups in the Bolshevist leadership broke out early in October, just before the Revolution. Two men in particular, Lev Kamenev and Grigori Zinoviev, opposed the violent seizure of power. Lenin shouted them down:

> Comrades, remember that two of the deserters, Kamenev and Zinoviev, showed themselves to be deserters and strike breakers even before the rising in Petrograd, because they not only voted against the rising at the decisive session of the Central Committee on October 10th, but agitated against the rising among Party officials after the Central Committee had passed the resolution. . . .

Whoever disagreed with Lenin was a deserter and a strike breaker; this was once again the Lenin of 1903, except that now he held power, even though that power was still very uncertain. This was demonstrated by the elections of 12th November for a Constituent Assembly, called by the Kerensky regime and then repeatedly deferred. The voting proved a devastating defeat for the Bolshevists in democratic terms; only a quarter of the thirty-six million electors voted for the Bolshevists, while nearly two thirds voted for the Social Revolutionaries. Out of 707 parliamentary seats, the Social Revolutionaries won 370, the Bolshevists only 175. Since he was now caught between an electoral defeat outside the Party, and sharp opposition within it, Lenin's position was critical. The war still continued at the front, and famine threatened in the rear. But Lenin's reaction was predictable, because he simply did not think in democratic terms. 'Only knaves and fools imagine that the proletariat must first obtain a majority through elections carried out under the bourgeois yoke and may only then try to seize power. . . .'

Machine-guns provided the accompaniment to the first session of the Constituent Assembly on 5th January 1918 in the Tauride Palace in Petrograd: Lenin's Party Guard was dispersing the crowd that had gathered in front of the building to acclaim the first freely elected parliament in Russian history. Lenin had appointed a swift end for it. His spokesman, Sverdlov, introduced a resolution demanding the immediate transfer of power to the Soviets; the parliament that had only just been elected should dissolve itself and place all authority in the hands of the Workers' and Soldiers' Councils. This was more than could be expected from a body in which the Bolshevists held only a quarter of the votes. The resolution was not even brought to the vote. By 237 votes to 138 the delegates present refused to place it at the top of the agenda. Thereupon, the Bolshevists walked out, followed by a small group of left-wing Social Revolutionaries. The Assembly remained legally competent to make decisions, but Lenin was determined to prevent it from doing so. The session proceeded amid an infernal din raised by the spectators in the gallery. Meanwhile, the machine-guns in front of the building claimed nearly a hundred victims. The second session never took place. On the next day the Tauride Palace had been occupied by troops. At the entrance two field-guns levelled their barrels at the elected representatives of the people.

Lenin had his own substitute Parliament ready. Four days after the violent end of the National Constituent Assembly, representatives of the Workers' and Soldiers' Councils, later joined by a delegation of Peasants' Representatives, gathered in Petrograd for the Third All-Russian Congress of Soviets. Lenin addressed them: 'Comrades! On behalf of the Council of People's Commissars I am called upon to report to you on its work during the two months and fifteen days which have gone by since the power of the Soviets and the Soviet Government were set up in Russia.' This was to be the first report on the Terror. Lenin justified the forceful dissolution of the elected Parliament: 'Not a single problem of the class struggle has been resolved during the course of history except by force. If force proceeds from the exploited working masses and against the exploiters – yes, then we are in favour of force.' The official account of the proceedings noted stormy applause. And Lenin continued: 'Therefore, comrades, to all complaints and accusations that we practice terror, dictatorship, civil war, we will reply – Yes, we have openly declared what no other government has ever been able to declare – yes, we have started the war against the exploiters'. And Lenin in his conclusion found the words needed to allay, in his own ranks, the fear of Terror. 'Let hundreds of strident voices hurl at us words such as dictatorship, violators, and the like – now there is no reason to fear the man with the rifle, because he defends the workers and will mercilessly strike down the rule of the exploiters!'

The true facts of the matter were made plain by Lenin's draft resolution for the Petrograd Soviet of 14th January 1918. After Parliament had been dispersed and there was no longer any representative central authority for the country as a whole the most urgent problems had to be solved by the use of force, since co-operation could hardly be expected from the people after popular representation had come to an end. Food was the most urgent problem of all, food for the capital before hunger drove the masses to acts of despair and the Council of Peoples' Commissars itself was swept away. So Lenin decreed that:

> The entire mass of soldiers and workers is to be mobilised with the object of forming several thousand sections (each of ten to fifteen men, or possibly more) whose duty it will be to devote a definite number of hours (for example three to four) to the procurement of food. . . .

The organisation for processing food was described:

> In the Revolutionary Sections, the most reliable and best-armed members shall be selected to carry out extraordinary measures for the prevention of famine, and despatched to all railway stations and to the administrative districts of the most important crop-producing provinces. These detachments shall be instructed to take the sharpest measures against speculators and for the requisitioning of harvest stocks.

In practice, this meant the organisation of marauding expeditions by heavily armed bands. Lenin remained true to his centralist principles – whoever held the capital held the whole country; therefore the country was to be mercilessly plundered in order to supply the capital with foodstuffs. As part of this undertaking, power over life and death was entrusted to these requisitioning detachments:

> Speculators who are caught red-handed and can be convicted on clear evidence will be executed on the spot by the detachments. When they draw up a report on an act of requisitioning, an arrest or an execution, the Revolutionary Sections will call upon at least six witnesses who must be picked from the poor population of the neighbourhood.

It was a simple and effective system. It was obvious that anyone with more than one loaf of bread on his shelf would come under suspicion as a speculator and that witnesses to rejoice over the liquidation of such rich folk would be easy enough to find among the poor. It was equally clear that the appeal to hunger and envy must turn the requisitioning troops into an army of murderous robbers which would inevitably attract the bitter hatred of those robbed. Such an army would be driven to practising merciless brutality, and thereby become an ever ready weapon for use by the central authorities, precisely what was needed to exercise Terror against the masses on behalf of a small minority. This army was the institution carefully created by Lenin for the application of Terror.

The institution was called the Cheka. On 7th December 1917, the Council of People's Commissars met to found the organisation which was to make the Terror a reality. It was to be called the 'All-Russian Extra-Ordinary Commission attached to the Council of People's Commissars of the R.S.F.S.R. for the Suppression of Counter Revolution, Espionage, Sabotage, Banditry, Black Marketing and Corruption'. The name is long and complicated. Instead the Party, which had retained a preference for abbreviations from its conspiratorial underground past, soon used the initials of the Commission's Russian title as a cipher for the new organisation: 'VTchK.' The Commission was an 'Organ of Central Authority' subordinate to the Council of People's Commissars as a whole, rather than to any particular People's Commissariat. The first organisational task was to create similar commissions for the individual republics, territories and towns. Their designation was 'TchK', and the Cheka was born.

Soon afterwards the Cheka became connected with a second symbol – the Lubyanka. This happened in the spring of 1918 when Lenin's Government left Petrograd and established the new capital in Moscow, mainly because the course of the war against Germany had brought the former centre of Government and the Government offices in Petrograd into dangerous proximity with the front line. The Cheka followed the Council of People's Commissars to Moscow. Its headquarters were housed in the former seat of an insurance company, at 22 Lubyanka Street. Its first regular unit, the nucleus of what were later to become the State Security Troops, was already in existence. It was a detachment of Latvian Sharpshooters which had joined the Soviets immediately after the October Revolution and had been brought to Petrograd by Lenin as a bodyguard shortly before the abolition of the Constituent Assembly.

On 20th December, the day on which the Council of People's Commissars founded the Cheka, Felix Dzerzhinsky, who had just been appointed its head, received a written instruction from Lenin: 'Concerning the Struggle against Counter-Revolutionaries and Saboteurs.' This instruction contained seven paragraphs, of which the most important are the first and the seventh.

> 1. Individuals belonging to the wealthy classes (i.e. those with a monthly income of five hundred roubles and more, owners of buildings and urban real estate, of shares and cash sums above one thousand roubles) as well as employees of banks, limited companies and Government and official institutions are bound to render to House Committees within twenty-four hours declarations in triplicate about their income, their place of work and their profession, stating their address and signed in their own hand. . . .
> 7. Persons who do not belong to the categories set out in paragraph 1 will hand to the House Committees one copy of a declaration about their income and their place of work and are obliged to carry on their person one copy of this declaration certified by the House Committee. . . .

Ostensibly the instruction was part of the preparations for the introduction of a General Labour Service. A sample Labour Book was attached to Lenin's letter. Members of the wealthy classes, including civil servants, were to enter details of their income and expenditure under the appropriate headings provided, and it was intended that House Committees, Works Committees and similar organisations should certify this information. In fact the instruction was the first to place an unbroken net of informers over the whole population. It was a subtly devised method of making every citizen watch every other citizen and to put the individual under permanent supervision at work and at home. It was also an appeal to the lowest human instincts, and to envy in particular. Every citizen was called upon to watch his neighbour with dislike and distrust, to peep at him through keyholes, to pursue him into the kitchen and the bedroom. This measure became the corner-stone of a Terror which nobody could evade. It made every citizen at once a suspect and an agent of the Cheka. Everyone watched everyone else and reported the results, if only to escape suspicion. And everybody could if necessary be turned into a witness who could not be contradicted.

The diabolical machinery which was to dominate the entire Soviet Union during the next decades was now in place. The mobilisation of armed units for plundering expeditions followed. Fear spread from the city to the whole land. Murder had been legalised. The Soviet State had found not only its Fouché and its Fouquier-Tinville, policeman and prosecutor in one person, but also its judge and executioner as well. The tremendous power which this system put into the hands of the man at the controls was obvious. Such a man could even threaten the People's Commissars who nominally stood above him. Lenin knew what he was doing when he chose Dzerzhinsky for the job, a man without personal ambition, an ascetic and in his own way a man of incorruptible rectitude.

Stalin, when he succeeded Lenin, kept Dzerzhinsky at his post, until his death in 1926. Thereafter, he could find nobody whom he could trust in the same way. His successor, Menzhinsky, was poisoned in May 1934.

Yagoda, who followed and who prepared the great Show Trials, was dismissed in 1936 and shot in 1938. The next man at the controls was Yezhov, who was forced to resign in 1938. He disappeared from the limelight without a trace. The last in the series of the omnipotent was Lavrenti Beria. He kept the post for fifteen years and outlived Stalin, only to be liquidated by Stalin's heirs in 1953. The Terror did not spare those who had served it. Sooner or later they were inevitably caught in their own web.

On 17th December 1919 *Pravda* published a set of theses by Trotsky. The man who only a few months after the October

Revolution virtually created the Red Army, now had some five million men under his command, and the end of the Civil War was in sight. On the North Front the 'White' General Yudenich, at one time near the suburbs of Petrograd, had been driven back. On the South Front the Red Army was advancing rapidly against the 'White' Commander-in-Chief, General Denikin, and the capture of Tzaritsyn seemed only a matter of days. In the East the most dangerous enemy of the Soviet regime, Admiral Kolchak, was in flight with his disintegrating army.

Trotsky could therefore well indulge in plans for the employment of his armies in peacetime. His proposals were simple but staggering. There was to be no demobilisation. The wartime organisation would be used to turn the entire male population into a labour force. The fighting armies were to become labour armies, and obligatory military service a General Labour Service. Taken to its logical conclusion Trotsky's plan meant that all Russia would become one gigantic forced labour camp.

Lenin and some of the other Soviet leaders accepted these proposals. Trotsky was appointed Chairman of a Commission for the introduction of a General Labour Service, but authoritarian ways had not yet become established among the Soviet leadership and Lenin and Trotsky met with bitter opposition. Their chief opponents were Rykov, later Chairman of the Council of People's Commissars, and the Labour Union leader Tomsky. Abramovich, a former Menshevik, spoke for many Bolsheviks when he said: 'They really cannot build a planned economy in the way in which the Pharaohs built the pyramids.'

This is indeed what Trotsky had in mind – the end of every freedom, including the proletarian's freedom to work, for the sake of the complete regimentation of manpower. He rejected the argument that forced labour is unproductive as a miserable and barren liberal prejudice, and went on to say: 'The forced labour of the serf was not the result of the feudal lord's ill-will. It was a progressive phenomenon.'

Such a position need not surprise anyone familiar with Bolshevik ways of thought. In fact, those who had once preached the freedom of labour were now talking about a 'workers' opposition'. By March 1921, when the Petrograd workers and the Kronstad sailors revolted against the Terror, Trotsky declared at the Tenth Party Congress:

The workers' opposition has launched dangerous slogans. It has made a fetish of democratic principles. It has, so to speak, put the right of the workers to elect representatives above that of the Party, as though the Party has no right to assert its dictatorship even when this dictatorship temporarily clashes with the passing mood of the workers' democracy. . . . The Party must assert its dictatorship regardless of any wavering in the temper of the masses, regardless of momentary losses of confidence within the working class. . . .

Trotsky failed to carry his proposals for a forced labour service against the majority of the delegates in 1921, but Stalin, the man destined to carry out his plans almost to the letter, was already standing by. Stalin had been Trotsky's chief representative in the Ukraine during the short period in 1919 when labour conscription had actually been in operation. Forced labour already had a clearly marked place in the Soviet system.

1. Sir Winston Churchill, *Memoirs of the Second World War* (Houghton Mifflin Company, Boston, 1959).
2. David Shub, *Lenin* (Doubleday, New York, 1948).

CHAPTER FOUR

The Infernal Machine

In the early evening of 6th July 1918 Felix Dzerzhinsky, the Head of the Cheka, was arrested in the Pokrovsky Barracks by the Cheka unit of Commissar Popov. The Social Revolutionaries had risen. Earlier on the same day two members of the Cheka called at the German Legation with a request signed by Dzerzhinsky that they should be received by the Minister, Count Mirbach. The request was a forgery.

Mirbach saw the visitors in the presence of the Councillor and the Military Attaché. One of the Cheka men pulled out his gun and fired several shots. Mirbach, wounded in the neck, managed to drag himself into a neighbouring room, but the other Chekist threw a grenade after him. Then both the murderers escaped through a window.

Soon afterwards Dzerzhinsky appeared at the Legation to conduct the investigation in person. During the days preceding the assassination a major clash had been brewing between the Bolsheviks and their last remaining non-Communist partners in the Government, the Left Social Revolutionaries. Dzerzhinsky knew that Popov had a high proportion of Social Revolutionaries in his unit and that he had recruited a group of former sailors notoriously opposed to the Bolsheviks from the Black Sea Fleet. Mirbach's murder gave Dzerzhinsky an excuse to intervene. He went straight from the Legation to the Pokrovsky Barracks without bothering to collect a strong escort and, gun in hand, requested Popov to surrender the two murderers. The sailors simply removed Dzerzhinsky's gun and declared him under arrest. A little later the Moscow Central Telegraph Office was occupied by members of Popov's unit who sent telegrams to every Soviet in the country announcing that Count Mirbach, 'the representative of German Imperialism', had been killed 'in accordance with a resolution of the Central Committee of the Social Revolutionaries', and that the latter had seized power. This proclamation by telegram virtually marked the end of the rising. Regular troops occupied the City centre. Latvian Sharpshooters surrounded the Bolshoi Theatre where the All-Russian Congress of Soviets was in session. A few rounds of artillery fired against the Pokrovsky Barracks dispersed Popov's unit and set Dzerzhinsky free. The Social Revolutionary delegates at the congress were locked into the cellars of the Bolshoi and a couple of dozen of their leaders were shot without trial.

July 1918 became a month of executions. The Commander of the Volga front, General Muraviev, a Social Revolutionary, had intended to march on Moscow and revive the rising. The army revolted and Muraviev was shot on 11th July by his own men led by their Political Commissar, who was to become Marshal Tukhachevsky. On 16th July the Tzar and his family were shot at Ekaterinburg. The Imperial family had been a source of great embarrassment to the Soviet Government. As long as it survived it represented a focus for attempts at a restoration, but it was thought unlikely that a public trial could result in the execution of children. Early in July anti-Bolshevik units were approaching Ekaterinburg. The evacuation of the Imperial family became impossible. The Ural Region Soviet decided that the Tzar, his wife and their children should be shot, together with a few members of their household. The extent to which the authorities in Moscow were involved in the decision to execute the Imperial family has never been fully clarified, but it is a remarkable coincidence at the very least that six other members of the Imperial family were killed a day later in a mine shaft at Alapaevsk, their place of exile in the Northern Ural Region.

Two other events further raised the tension. The head of the Leningrad Cheka, Uritsky, was shot by a young officer on 30th August. On the same day, a Social Revolutionary, Fanya Kaplan, approached Lenin in the street with a petition, drew a gun from her shopping basket and wounded him slightly in the chest and shoulder. The Social Revolutionaries disclaimed responsibility for this attempt, as opposed to Mirbach's murder. Uritsky's murderer was not a Social Revolutionary. But the two events showed that resistance to the Bolshevik regime was building up to an explosion. The regime struck back quickly: Mass Terror against all enemies of the Soviet State was proclaimed on 3rd September 1918.

Six weeks before his misadventure in the Pokrovsky Barracks

Dzerzhinsky had written to his wife in Switzerland: 'I have been posted in the first line of fire and I am determined to fight, to face the full danger of a threatening situation and to be extremely ruthless in mauling the enemy like a faithful watchdog.' At this point of time Mass Terror in the full sense still lay in the future. What had happened so far was normal in any revolution. When the sailors mutinied in Kronstadt in February 1917 they literally tore their admiral to pieces. Dukhonin, the last Commander-in-Chief, was murdered by soldiers who had merely been told to arrest him. These and many other similar cases had little or nothing to do with ideologies or policies. There was also nothing unprecedented about the wholesale execution of the rebels after Mirbach's murder or the shooting of 512 prisoners without trial after the killing of Uritsky and the attempted assassination of Lenin. Events such as these belong to a typical revolutionary pattern, but on 3rd September the pattern changed radically. The People's Commissariat of Internal Affairs addressed an instruction to all Soviets which was published in *Izvestia* the next day:

> The murder of Volodarsky, the murder of Uritsky, the attempted assassination of the Chairman of the Council of People's Commissars, V. I. Lenin, the mass shooting of tens of thousands of our comrades in Finland and the Ukraine, as well as on the Don and in Czechoslovakia, the discovery of constantly renewed attacks against the rear of our armies, the open participation of Right Social Revolutionaries and other counter-revolutionary scoundrels in these plots, taken together with the exceptionally low number of serious counter-measures and mass executions of White Guards and bourgeois by the Soviets, show that in spite of all the constant talk about a Mass Terror against Social Revolutionaries, White Guards and the bourgeoisie this Terror does not, in fact, exist.
>
> An end must be put once and for all to this state of affairs. Laxity and weakness must cease. All Social Revolutionaries known to the local Soviets must be arrested immediately. A significant number of members of the bourgeoisie and officers must be taken as hostages. At the slightest sign of resistance and whenever any White Guard shows any sign of activity mass executions are to be undertaken. Local Provincial Executive Committees must display particular initiative in this respect. Local authorities must take all measures in conjunction with the Militia and the Extraordinary Commission to ensure that all those sheltering under false identities are discovered and arrested and that any of these who have been involved in White Guard activities are unconditionally shot.
>
> All these measures must be carried out immediately.
>
> The Commissariat of Internal Affairs is to be informed immediately

if local Soviets show any lack of energy in this respect. Finally, all traces of White Guard activity and foul plotting against the power of the working class and the poorest peasants in the rear of our Army must be eliminated. There must be no delay or hesitation in the application of the Mass Terror. . . .

This instruction may read like the ranting of some demented Anarchist, but it bears the signature of Petrovsky, the People's Commissar of Internal Affairs. It is the only instance in history of a Government invitation to its officials and the local authorities, from the capital to the smallest village, to make murder the basis of administration. The mayor of every village was instructed to shoot without investigation a fellow citizen who aroused his suspicions. Conversely, every citizen was instructed to denounce the mayor if he felt that the latter was not ordering enough executions. As from 3rd September 1918 the Party officials were invited to a head-hunt against the whole population of Russia.

The resulting number of victims can only be estimated very roughly. The Cheka officially reported 12,733 executions between 1918 and 1921. Between the end of 1918 and mid-1919, 8,389 executions were reported for Central Russia, on the following grounds: participation in rebellions – 3,082; membership of counter-revolutionary organisations – 2,024; gangsterism – 643; incitement to revolution – 455; corruption – 206; espionage – 102; desertion – 102. Other unspecified crimes accounted for 1,704 executions. There is no means of telling how closely these figures approximate to the facts. They refer only to Cheka activities and give no indication of the number of people executed by local authorities. Some 5,000 executions from the beginning of the Mass Terror to the end of the Civil War seems a reasonable estimate, apart from the hundreds of thousands who died as a result of military operations.

Three weeks after Petrovsky's call to Terror, Dzerzhinsky, who was responsible for implementing it, wrote to his wife in Switzerland:

> There is a sort of stillness in our building today. Vague depression, sadness, nostalgia for the past – a longing burdens the soul. Today – perhaps it is a matter of being tired – I do not want to think about business. . . . My room is quite empty and silent and I feel your presence as I used to do in prison. I am there even now. I dream. I should like to be a poet in order to sing the song of life and love. . . .

Even Dzerzhinsky was at the end of his tether, and a few weeks later set out for Switzerland to recuperate with his family.

It was the task of Georgi Chicherin, People's Commissar of Foreign Affairs, to justify the organised massacre to world opinion. This former Tzarist diplomat turned revolutionary, a short-sighted, fussy hypochondriac in a crumpled tweed suit bought when he was an émigré in London, had to face sharp protests by the neutral powers represented in Moscow, Petrograd and the larger cities. Chicherin replied by counter-attacking 'the regime of White Terror against the working class throughout the capitalist world'. He wrote:

> The Russian working class will pitilessly suppress the counter-revolutionary gang which, supported by foreign capital and the Russian middle class, would like to trap the Russian people in the snare of war and slavery. We declare before the proletariat of the world at large that we will not allow ourselves to be deflected by sanctimonious protests and petitions from punishing those who take up arms against the workers and the poor peasants of Russia. . . . We know that the masses of every country who are oppressed and terrorised by small groups of exploiters will understand that violence is only applied in Russia in the holy cause of human liberty, and that they will not merely understand but will follow our example.

Not only did the Soviet rulers proclaim Mass Terror against their own citizens as a method of government: they triumphantly told the rest of the world about it and invited it to follow suit.

Dzerzhinsky could only take two weeks of his leave in Switzerland in 1918. The Cheka required reorganisation. Something more orderly and durable was needed in the place of the hastily created 'Extra-ordinary Commission'.

The successful Russian revolutionaries were confronted by two unusual problems in setting up a political police force. As a rule, revolutionary movements are driven to using the very men who repressed them earlier, and many police officials, being professional Government servants and anxious to survive, have often been only too glad to collaborate. There could be no question of this after the Bolsheviks had seized power, if only because the rapid changes of government after the abdication of the Tzar had eliminated too many professional policemen.

The real problem, however, arose because the Bolshevik leaders were utterly ignorant of the routine of government, while their supporters lacked any political and managerial experience. If the State and its economy were to go on functioning, the co-operation of at least the middle and lower echelons of the trained and educated was required.

Things were bad enough in the Army. The February Revolution had stripped the officers of their authority, while the war continued and a civil war followed. Occasionally, born leaders emerged, such as Semen Budenny, a top sergeant in a Cossack regiment in 1917 and a general by the next summer, but such cases were exceptional. Trotsky was soon forced to recruit every Tzarist officer willing to serve the new regime. Government servants, managers, engineers had to be left in their jobs but it was clear that neither the former officers nor the bureaucrats could be expected to become reliable Bolsheviks overnight. They might not desire the restoration of Tzarism, but they all hoped for some liberalisation and democratisation of life.

Dzerzhinsky and his brand new Security Service therefore had to keep virtually the whole class of managerial and government workers under constant supervision, as well as the Army officers. The leaders of this Security Service were professional revolutionaries and may have learned something in prison from the Okhrana, but the rank and file of the Cheka were nothing more than ordinary workers and peasants who had proved their reliability in the Party. In any case, these men, numerous as they were, could not control the entire population of Russia. Dzerzhinsky needed completely reliable shock troops at his disposal. He had to reckon with widespread popular revolts and it was always doubtful in the early years whether the regular army would obey orders in such cases. Cheka troops had to stand by to suppress possible mutinies in the Red Army.

The first Cheka troops to be organised on a regular basis were the so-called Special Assignment Units, ChON, forty battalions to guard important objectives, as well as a permanent reserve for the suppression of internal disturbances. They were followed by the VOKhR and VNUS, Internal Security and Internal Service Troops assigned to various branches of Government. By 1919 these troops comprised 100,000 men under the People's Commissariat of Internal Affairs; in an emergency they were to be directly subordinated to the Cheka. In fact, Dzerzhinsky became People's Commissar of Internal Affairs in 1919.

In its early days a number of disreputable characters had found their way into the Cheka. It was a fruitful field of activity for criminals: house searches could lead to theft, requisitioning could become plunder and orders for arrest could be used for black-mail. The first wave of purges in the Security organisation, in July and August 1918, aimed not only at Social Revolutionaries but also at criminals. Dzerzhinsky was completely incorruptible and the Mass Terror proclaimed in September must have troubled his conscience, since arrests and requisitioning often concealed private acts of vengeance. A 'Special Tribunal' of the Cheka was set up, operating in secret, independently of the regular civil and military courts, and principally to bring arbitrary executions under control. The Special Tribunal was not bound by legal procedures or statutes. There was no public prosecutor, and the Cheka acted as both attorney and judge. The accused were not allowed to call on defence counsel. Sentence was at the discretion of the members of the tribunal.

The Special Tribunal later became a 'Judicial Board', and eventually turned into the Special Councils which were among Stalin's most effective instrument of Terror.

The 'Hot Terror' – the Terror aimed at defeating the counter-revolutionaries – ended in 1921. Between 1918 and 1921 many of the non-Russian nationalities on the borders of the old empire had declared themselves independent. There were White Armies everywhere. The Germans occupied the Ukraine for a time. The British were in the North and in the Caucasian oil fields. Some fifty thousand French troops were in Southern Russia. The Japanese and the Americans ruled Eastern Siberia. Disunited as they were among themselves, these foreign troops had the over-throw of Bolshevism as their common aim. Even when the Allies withdrew, the Red Army still had to knock out one group of opponents of the regime after another. There may have been little to be said in favour of a regime established by violence and maintained in power by unrivalled brutality, but the 'Hot Terror' was a matter of self-defence for a government threatened on every side. The Cheka's role in the area under the effective control of Moscow was to break up conspiracies and spread an atmosphere of fear which would check any thought of resistance among the population.

The external threat vanished in 1921 with the end of the Civil

War. The internal enemy, however, continued to exist: the intelligentsia and the managerial classes who had expected an increase in personal and political liberties; the peasantry, liberated from feudalism merely to be subjected to a system of forced delivery of agricultural produce at fixed prices; and the national minorities who detested the centralist Bolshevik Government in Moscow as much as they had hated the Imperial regime in Petersburg. The internal enemy, in fact, comprised the majority of a population increasingly dissatisfied with a regime that could fulfil only few of its great promises. After nearly seven years of economic disorganisation and physical destruction food and clothes were scarce. There were no machines to make consumer goods and there was no industry to make the machines. The 'People' for whose sake the Revolution had allegedly been made were hardly better off anywhere in Russia, and in many places the average worker and the average peasant were a great deal worse off than in 1914. This was by no means entirely the fault of the regime, but the regime had promised to create a paradise on earth. Now Bolshevism faced the disillusionment of the masses. Moreover, the leaders knew very well that the promises made when they achieved power would take many more years to fulfil. And so the Cheka remained a necessity, no longer as a means of self-defence for the State against an external threat, but as a weapon against the population. This instrument was re-named GPU in 1922.

In December 1922 Russia became the Union of Socialist Soviet Republics under a new constitution. In theory this was a federation based on the free association of independent states and the right of national self-determination, a convenient formula since other nations could in future join the Union without the need for formal annexation. In reality, the world revolution did not spread as planned, and annexations followed. The liquidation of the Baltic States, the incorporation of Bessarabia, of parts of Finland, Poland and Czechoslovakia, the occupation of parts of East Prussia and the annexation of Tannutuva on the Mongolian border were all straightforward acts of military and political conquest.

    The realities of free association in the Union are well illustrated by the reorganisation of the Security system. The People's

Commissariat of Internal Affairs (which is abbreviated in Russian as NKVD) was one of the first and most powerful People's Commissariats – in other words, ministries – created by the Bolsheviks when they came to power. But according to the constitution the Union Republics were free from central interference in their internal affairs. The NKVD was dissolved and each Union Republic acquired a Commissariat of the Interior of its own. The Security Service however remained a central organisation – 'The United State Political Directorate Attached to the Council of People's Commissars of the Union of Socialist Soviet Republics', or, more briefly, 'OGPU attached to the SNK of the USSR'. At first there was an OGPU representative in each Union Republic, then State Political Directorates were established for each Republic. Every GPU office was directly subordinate to the OGPU in Moscow, and not the local authorities.

The definition of the OGPU's responsibility was brief and to the point: 'The struggle against political and economic counter-revolution, espionage and banditism.' As there was no counter-revolution worth mentioning after 1921, the definition requires some comment. Counter-revolution meant any word or deed directed against the regime. Espionage embraced every communication of official, technical, scientific and military information abroad or to organisations or persons hostile to the regime. Banditism covered every form of armed action or violent resistance. These concepts could be extended indefinitely to cover the most harmless activities. A man could become a spy if he discussed his work, whatever its nature, with anyone who might come to be considered hostile to the regime. Any expression of opinion, however harmless or insignificant, might be treated as counter-revolutionary activity because, the definition of hostility to the State varied with the extent to which the regime felt insecure.

A very recent instance of this elasticity in defining the threat to the regime is the sentence of seven and five years of forced labour passed in February 1966 on two Soviet writers, Andrei Sinyavsky and Yuri Daniel, for writing satires about conditions in the Soviet Union which they allowed to be published abroad. The case, and its absurdly severe sentences, provoked a wave of protest which could not be entirely disregarded by the Soviet authorities, since even foreign Communists joined in it. If such acts of repression can still occur in the late sixties it is easy to imagine what went on in the twenties and thirties when the GPU was at the height of its power. Then as now there appear to be two main elements in such security measures: the fears of a shaky régime faced with hostile activities the importance of which it tends grossly to overrate; and the determination to spread fear among those who might otherwise be tempted to indulge in such activities.

The Head of the OGPU was appointed by the Praesidium of the Executive Committee of the Supreme Soviet, and attended the Council of People's Commissars in a consultative capacity. Supervision of the legality of the OGPU's activities was the responsibility of the General Prosecutor's office of the Supreme Court of the Soviet Union, of which an OGPU representative was also a member. As the Soviet judiciary was no more than an instrument of the dictatorship throughout the Stalin era, this legal supervision of GPU activities was a mere formality. In any case the GPU's brief was so broad in its statement of the crimes covered that all its actions could be shown to be legal.

The special judicial powers of the Cheka passed to the GPU and the Head of the OGPU became the Chairman of its Tribunal. The regular members of the Security Service were recruited from the graduates of special three-year courses and from the most promising officers at the Frunze Military Academy.

The activities of the GPU gradually covered the whole country and, particularly after Stalin had established his rule, even included the supervision of Party officials right to the very top. Eventually there was a GPU representative in every larger economic enterprise and in every Party and Government office, quite apart from those operating under cover. The latter complemented the information available to the GPU and were used to keep an eye on the official GPU representatives.

As more and more foreign countries recognised the Soviet regime, exchanged diplomatic and consular representatives with it, received or sent economic missions and developed cultural contacts, a new field and new opportunities opened for the GPU. It is wrong to regard all Soviet activities abroad as to some extent subversive. It would be equally wrong not to recognise that Soviet missions abroad maintain contacts with agents, saboteurs and members of the Communist Party in the host countries. These contacts usually came under the executive control of the GPU agents acting as Secretaries in diplomatic missions, commercial delegates and travel agents. Of course, this sort of behaviour is not a Russian monopoly. The secret services of the Western democracies operate in the same way and claim that they do so to protect their régimes and the liberty of their fellow citizens. The Soviet authorities also claim that their secret service is defending the achievements of Socialism. In practice, however, the Soviet Secret Service has distinguished itself from the start by its thoroughness, by the depth of the penetration it has achieved, by the quality of its training and its success. The incomparably greater effectiveness of the Soviet Secret Service is the direct result of the system under which it operates. The secret services of the Western democracies must continually battle with parliamentary commissions and take account of public opinion. The Soviet service, on the other hand, works without supervision or, at any rate, is supervised only by professionals in its own field. Its financial resources are virtually unlimited and no parliamentary representative is likely to ask embarrassing questions about its budget.

The Soviet Secret Service had these advantages from the time when Felix Dzerzhinsky reorganised the GPU for peace-time work. He was not destined to see it reach technical perfection under Stalin's dictatorship. He died peacefully in bed – the last holder of his post to do so for many years – and was succeeded by his deputy, Vyacheslav Menzhinsky.

CHAPTER FIVE

The Perfect Confession

In 1934, the Smolny Institute in Leningrad, which had been a monastery, then a college for young ladies and, during the Revolution, the Bolshevik headquarters, housed the city's Communist Party Committee and its First Secretary, Sergei Kirov. Kirov was one of the most powerful leaders in the Communist Party together with Stalin, one of the three Secretaries of the Central Committee. He was generally regarded as Stalin's favourite and his successor designate.

Leonid Nikolaev, a former Party member recently expelled for deviationism, visited the Institute towards the end of that year. He was stopped in one of the corridors, was searched and arrested for carrying a gun, and taken to the Deputy Head of the local NKVD, Zaporozhets. According to normal NKVD practice the best he could expect was a bullet in the back of the neck. Instead, he was released. A few days later the Smolny guard again arrested him for carrying a weapon and brought him to Zaporozhets, who released him once more. On 1st December 1934 he succeeded in eluding the guard on his third visit. Kirov was walking alone down a corridor despite the strict instruction to the bodyguards of all senior officials never to let them out of their sight. Nikolaev fired and Kirov fell dead.

The murder was investigated by Stalin, Molotov and Voroshilov in person. The first question was how Kirov's bodyguard came to be absent at the crucial moment. The truck in which the bodyguard was being taken for interrogation swerved, according to the driver, because the NKVD official sitting beside him knocked the wheel out of his hand. It hit a wall. The prisoner's two escorts reported that he had been killed in the accident. They were both shot and the bodyguard's failure to protect Kirov remained a mystery.

Nikolaev testified at his trial that Zaporozhets, the Deputy Head of the Leningrad NKVD, had recruited him to assassinate Kirov and had provided the weapon. Nikolaev was sentenced to death and shot. Zaporozhets, his immediate superior and eight other NKVD officials were only sentenced to a few years of imprisonment, but two years later they were shot without trial.

For twenty years the details of Kirov's murder were shrouded in rumour and mystery. A suspicion lingered that Stalin himself had a hand in the crime. This explanation of the chain of events, whereby those principally involved were conveniently eliminated one after the other, was first officially mentioned in Khrushchev's Secret Speech at the Twentieth Party Congress.

Immediately after the murder it was announced that 'unknown White Guards had killed the favourite of the masses'. Nikolaev and thirteen others were indicted at the trial as members of an alleged Leningrad Terrorist Centre and of a Left Oppositionist group, and the accused had indeed been excluded from the Party on account of deviations to the left. Nikolaev believed that by murdering Kirov he could draw the attention of the whole Soviet Union to the 'bureaucratic degeneration of the Party leadership'. This might well have suited Stalin by providing a welcome excuse for a wholesale purge of the Party to the very top. This removal of the Old Bolsheviks and of every vestige of collective leadership in order to establish the dictatorship of the Chief over the Party became known as the Great Purge.

The origins of the Great Purge go back to Lenin's first stroke in 1922. He had been the undisputed leader of the Party, but mild as dictators go. He never attempted to expel the other members of the Party leadership, to intimidate his colleagues in the Politburo or to restrict their freedom of speech. Within the leadership he worked by persuasion, not violence, subject to the basic Bolshevik rule that when a decision had been taken by the Politburo, members of any minority must give whole-hearted support to it. Lenin was also willing to forgive and forget. He buried his old feud with Trotsky during the preparations for the October Revolution. He very soon took Zinoviev and Kamenev, who had opposed the armed rising, back into favour and never referred to his description of them at the time as deserters and strike-breakers.

After May 1922 Lenin's hold over the Party began to falter. His health improved at times, but he never completely recovered. He returned to Moscow in October 1922 but suffered another stroke in December. From then until his death in January 1924 he stayed at Gorki and only conducted business by letter.

One of these letters only reached the addressees – the Party as a whole – thirty years later, at the Twentieth Party Congress. It was intended as a guidance to the Twelfth Party Congress in 1923. 'Having become General Secretary, Comrade Stalin has concentrated enormous power in his hands, and I am not sure that he always knows how to use that power with sufficient caution', and further: 'Stalin is too rude. . . . Therefore I suggest to the comrades that they should find a way to remove Stalin from that position.'

This letter has since become known as Lenin's political testament. Its very existence was the focus of intrigues among the men at the top of the Party for many years. Nobody dared to publish it, not even Stalin's opponents – it might have led to open conflict and the breaking up of the Party. That was too great a risk for people to whom the Party was virtually the sole reason for existence. Lenin's wife kept silent. Trotsky even denied the existence of the letter when information about it leaked out. It was used as a means of pressure among the contending members of the leadership, but when Trotsky was finally driven to using it publicly he was defeated by his own earlier denials.

It would be an over-simplification to regard the fight for Lenin's succession between 1923 and 1927 as merely a power struggle. It was also a passionate debate about how the country, brought to the brink of economic ruin by war, revolution and civil war, could be put on its feet again. In Communist terms it was a matter of finding the right way to socialism.

Quite apart from the differing points of view and attitudes of the individuals involved, a deep personal gulf separated the old Bolsheviks from Stalin, in addition to the disagreements about doctrine and practice which divided the leaders. Stalin was a Georgian cobbler's son, a practical revolutionary without higher education, ignorant of foreign languages and without real experience of conditions outside Russia.

When the Revolution broke out Lenin already had twenty-five thick volumes of collected works to his credit. When Stalin's collected works were published two slender volumes covered all the years up to 1917. Lenin, Trotsky, Zinoviev, Kamenev, Bukharin were intellectuals, inspired theoreticians, brilliant writers, nimble debaters, while Stalin's grasp in these matters was rudimentary. Between them the others had travelled half the globe, while Stalin was spending his time in Tzarist prisons and places of exile in Siberia. Trotsky, Zinoviev and Kamenev were Jews and Stalin never entirely rid himself of the anti-semitism, inspired by envy and vague suspicion, that is so deeply rooted among the lower classes of Eastern Europe. Lenin was a lawyer, Bukharin a university teacher, Trotsky the son of a landowner and Kamenev the son of an engineer, while Stalin had got no further than working as an assistant in an observatory. As long as the debate ranged over points of theory and ideology Stalin was bound to feel inferior to his opponents.

The others, however, lacked his supreme organisational talent developed in the struggles of the Russian underground. He was a model of Lenin's professional revolutionary. Trotsky was also a brilliant organiser but he spent himself in creating the Red Army, while Stalin was building up the Party organisation. In the struggle between them Stalin could win by means of the Party, while Trotsky could only start another civil war.

The debate centred on two basic problems, the question of nationalities and economic policy. In theory, the question of nationalities had been solved by the constitution which created the Union Republics. In practice, Makharadze – a Georgian representative at the Twelfth Party Congress in April 1923 – described the situation accurately when he said that talk about independence was meaningless: in the last resort it was the central Party which 'decides everything for every republic'.

The debate over economic policy went even deeper: should the emphasis be on heavy industry or on agriculture, should there be bread or machines? The left wing, with Trotsky, Zinoviev and Kamenev, advocated the promotion of heavy industry and industrialisation at all costs, including compulsion in the country-side to secure food to the industrial workers. The right wing, led by Bukharin, considered that the peasants should retain their freedom and their ownership of the land and that they should be induced to deliver food by an increase in their earnings.

Stalin's position was to the right with regard to the peasants, and to the left on the question of nationalities, less as a matter of principle than to secure room for manœuvre. He was determined to be as ruthless as necessary whenever this was possible, as in the question of nationalities. Whenever force was unlikely to succeed he was willing to back down, at any rate for the time being, as in the case of the peasants.

The Party was also divided over the World Revolution. Trotsky was its chief proponent and Zinoviev and Kamenev also clung to the idea. These 'leftists' believed that as long as the Soviet Union represented a foreign body in a largely capitalist world it would be unable to solve its own problems. Any suggestion of socialism in a single country seemed absurd to them. Stalin was more practical. He had realised for some time that the World Revolution which was supposed to be imminent should be written off for the present. There were no real signs of it. Even Germany had disappointed Communist hopes. In spite of all theories to the contrary, it was clearly essential to establish socialism in the Soviet Union, at least if the Bolsheviks were to survive. Stalin was able to brand the 'leftists' as cowards and opportunists, and to accuse them of underrating the strength of the Russian proletariat. By opting for 'Socialism in One Country' Stalin found further favour with the majority of the Party's rank and file. Trotsky was forced to tell them clearly and forcefully that without the World Revolution they could achieve no lasting success, while Stalin assured them that they could succeed alone and by their own efforts.

And so the battle, which eventually resulted in the Great Purge, was at first waged in the upper reaches of the Party by means of quotations from the Communist scriptures. In those authoritarian regimes which rely on a dogma, opposition is beaten down with texts from the authorised scriptures. There is no arguing against a doctrine once it had been proclaimed, and so it was in the Soviet Union between Lenin's death and the Fifteenth Party Congress in December 1927. However, as the moment of decision approached the principals in the battle were no longer content to leave it at that. Zinoviev mobilised his supporters in the Leningrad Party Organisation. Leningrad was still the greatest industrial centre in the country and its hungry workers were easily aroused against attempts to favour the peasants. Local patriotism also came into play – the inhabitants of the former capital resented the down-grading of Leningrad to mere provincial status.

Unity could no longer be restored within the Party leadership after the Fourteenth Congress in December 1925. The Leningrad group was out-voted, but not won over. Kamenev thundered during the plenary session: 'I have come to the conclusion that Comrade Stalin is unable to fulfil the part of unifier of the Bolshevik general staff. We are opposed to the doctrine of rule by a single individual, we are against the creation of a leader.' This was the left opposition's slogan for the next two years while it elaborated its ideological platform: emphasis on heavy industry and improvement of the workers' living conditions; control over the peasants and their prosperity which was increasing at the expense of the urban population; mobilisation of the Communist International to bring about World Revolution.

In October 1926 Trotsky, Zinoviev and Kamenev found themselves in a minority in the Central Committee. Trotsky and Kamenev were excluded from the Politburo and Zinoviev had to surrender his key position as Chairman of the Comintern. These three now took the desperate step of forming a dissident fraction, a mortal sin against Bolshevik dogma. The formation of groups and fractions had been banned by the Tenth Party Congress in 1921. At the Thirteenth Party Congress in May 1924 Stalin defended himself against a ferocious attack by Trotsky by referring to this rule and was given an ovation by loyal Party officials. A Commission of Inquiry later set up under Dzerzhinsky's chairmanship to examine the question of democracy within the Party called for the intensification of the struggle against deviationists. It became the duty of every member to inform the GPU of any attempt to create groups. To promote fractions was an even worse crime: it implied canvassing for a group and its independent platform. In 1927 the Trotsky-Zinoviev-Kamenev group actually tried to put their platform before the mass of the Party membership. In the meantime Lenin's political testament had been sent abroad by Lenin's widow and was published in full by the *New York Times* on 18th October 1926.

By the end of 1927 the Soviet Union seemed to be on the brink of civil war. Trotsky had set up an illegal printing press in order to publish his platform – for wide circulation. On the tenth Anniversary of the October Revolution Zinoviev organised demonstrations in Moscow and Leningrad which verged on rioting. The GPU struck back; it had not been asleep while the first, cold phase of the Purge was being fought out by means of texts and declarations of principle. Trotsky's and Zinoviev's groups had long been penetrated by GPU agents. The press was closed down and the demonstrations in Moscow and Leningrad were dispersed by the police.

The masses did not rise. Lenin's doctrine that power could only be seized by an army of professional revolutionaries was again vindicated: as long as the Party machine remained in Stalin's hands there could be no rebellion against him.

Zinoviev and Kamenev capitulated after ninety-three delegates had been expelled for opposition from the Fifteenth Party Congress. They abjectly confessed their faults and petitioned for re-admission to the Party. Trotsky refused to sign the petition and the Soviet public was informed on 28th January 1928 that he had left Moscow with some of his friends. Exile to Siberia was back in fashion.

The moment was not yet ripe for the physical liquidation of opponents, but the necessary preparations were in hand. The Lubyanka archives were bursting with material for use at a moment's notice whenever Stalin might feel that his hold over the Party was weakening. Dzerzhinsky, and Menzhinsky after him, had laid the foundations for the hot phase of the Great Purge and worked out techniques of complete confession as a preparation for the perfect trial.

In November 1922 Georg Popoff, a journalist of Russian descent but a German citizen, was arrested in Moscow. His friendship with Chicherin, the People's Commissar of Foreign Affairs, and Radek, the General Secretary of the Third International, caused him to be much in demand as a correspondent for European and American newspapers, which even then found it difficult to obtain first hand material from the Soviet Union.

Popoff was taken from the Savoy Hotel to the Lubyanka, No. 2, once the shop of the greengrocer Ovanesov. Ovanesov's shop, as it was still known, was a place which everybody in Russia preferred to avoid.

Among the thousands who passed through it in those early days, Georg Popoff was unique because he was the first to publish his reminiscences abroad, in 1925 – long before the flood of memoirs by other victims of Soviet Security which provide a clear and detailed picture of the methods used by the Cheka and its successors.

Popoff's ordeal began with his interrogation by GPU official Skrodsky:[1]

'A man who is totally loyal to us, a dedicated Communist, has reported from Berlin the details of your contacts there and the plans which you have brought to Moscow. We have not the slightest reason for distrusting our representative. As a simple worker, I again advise you to confess of your own free will and we will then release you this very day.'

'I cannot confess to what has not happened.'

'So you wish to go on denying?'

'I have told you the whole truth.'

The interrogation went round in a circle for some time until Popoff finally said:

'Generally speaking I am delighted that such absurdities should have been the reason for my arrest. You should find it easy to convince yourself of my innocence. I feel really relieved, as I thought that God knows what accusations would be made against me!'

Skrodsky, who had clearly been waiting for an unguarded word from me, pounced with the agility of a lurking beast of prey: 'So!' he exclaimed ironically, 'you are pleased that such insignificant things are being held against you, and you feel relieved? Then there must be something that you have concealed and which has been weighing on your conscience!'

The next interrogation was conducted by a man called Roller who had a reputation among the prisoners of being particularly 'sharp'. This time new names of alleged conspirators were brought in:

'You therefore deny the fact that you have conspired in Berlin with Baron Taube and General Lerond?'

'There is nothing to deny, because I have neither seen nor met the gentlemen concerned.'

'We have proof of the contrary.'

'I do not know what your proof amounts to and you may, after all, be mistaken.'

'The Cheka never makes a mistake.'

The third interrogation was conducted by Artusov, whom Popoff describes as smooth and silky.

'And so you still maintain that, as you told Comrade Roller, Baron Taube was not present during your conversation with General Lerond?'

Returning Artusov's dark look, I answered as quietly as possible:

'Comrade Artusov, you seem to be misinformed. I have told Comrade Roller several times that I have met neither the one nor the other, and I stand by this.'

'Quite, quite – please forgive me, I had momentarily misread the report.'

Then Artusov asked me to sit down again and said: 'It is probable that we will release you after a while. But we must ask for one thing straightaway – if you later meet Comrade Chicherin, Comrade Radek or any other member of the Soviet Government, please do not enlarge on the subjects which we have been discussing.'

'I am sorry – I do not understand you,' I answered with deliberate naivety. 'Do you mean that I should say nothing in conversation with Radek, Chicherin and other Soviet leaders of my acquaintance about the true reasons for my arrest, in other words about your accusation that I have conspired with Baron Taube, General Lerond and others against the Soviet authorities?'

'That is correct. Of course we would not give you orders. But we believe it might be better . . .'

'But that is hardly possible. What am I to tell Comrade Radek if he asks me why I was arrested?'

'Tell him simply it was a misunderstanding over your passport, about forbidden dealing in gem stones or suspicious concourse with monarchists – anything at all. . . .'

At the fourth interrogation Roller appeared again. Nothing more was said about the alleged conspiracy. Instead a declaration of loyalty appeared on the interrogator's table.

'We have realised,' Roller assured me in a friendly way, 'that we have made a mistake about you. We have no doubt about your loyalty. You do not harbour any hostile intentions against us, do you?'

'Of course not! You know that very well!'

'Splendid! Then you are certainly also prepared to confirm this for us in writing as a matter of form?'

'Any time.'

'Very well. So, please write!'

And Roller dictated the following declaration to me:

'I the undersigned hereby declare that I have not undertaken any hostile act against the existing order in Russia and that I am thoroughly loyal to the Soviet authorities. In proof of this, if any plans prepared to organise counter-revolutionary circles against the Soviet Government come to my knowledge, I undertake immediately to report the fact to the State Political Directorate (GPU), and also to carry out their orders.'

I said to Comrade Roller: 'What you have just dictated is nothing less than an obligation to serve the Cheka.'

Roller pretended to be indignant: 'Certainly not,' he replied. 'This has nothing to do with serving the Cheka. In fact, it is only a formality. Comrade Dzerzhinsky has shown exceptional interest for your case. He has kept himself informed of all its details, and it is the express wish of Comrade Dzerzhinsky that you should sign this declaration exactly as I have dictated it to you.'

I was pleased that I had at least succeeded in forcing Comrade Roller into this admission. He explicitly confirmed once again that I would be released as soon as I had signed the declaration. So I took up the pen and signed what was in front of me, which was as good as signing away one's soul to the devil . . .

But disappointment was in store for me. There was no question of release. Instead there began what was known in Lubyanka jargon as the 'major battle', a massive attempt finally to break down a prisoner expecting his release. For this purpose Roller was again the interrogator.

'Now this is the position,' began Roller in a tone that suggested that he was talking about a wholly minor matter. 'A formal report of your arrest must be drawn up. Any reference to Baron Taube, General Lerond and the rest would, for political reasons, be most undesirable from our point of view. I have thoroughly discussed this point with Comrade Dzerzhinsky. He considers it would be best if we said that you had been arrested for attempted trading in gem stones and had later been cleared and released, after proving your innocence in this respect.'

There had indeed been a technical offence involving precious stones. Popoff had taken a friend to an antique dealer he knew. The GPU clearly knew about this from the start, which showed how closely Popoff had been watched before he was arrested. As Popoff considered that there was nothing criminal about this deal, he admitted everything without hesitation.

His 'confession' ended as follows:

'I admit that I was involved as a middle-man in the sale of a diamond weighing roughly 10 carats by the commission agent Jacobson to the antique dealer Vladimirov. I was not aware at the time that the purchase and sale of gem stones was forbidden by law in the Soviet Union. I acted in the honest belief that I was doing nothing illegal.'

Hardly had Roller finished reading this document before a glint of triumph appeared in his eye. He shut the file containing my report with a bang, laid it in front of him on the table, glanced at me in an entirely different, half threatening, half bullying way and said cuttingly: 'You are now in our power! You have just testified in writing that you have committed a crime under Soviet law, and punishable as such. Apart from this you rate as our agent and a Soviet citizen on the strength of your declaration of loyalty. If you do not now finally admit what you have plotted against the Soviet authorities with Baron Taube, General Lerond and other scoundrels, the Board of the Cheka will sentence you to ten years of forced labour in Archangel for illicit trading in gems, and may you die there!'

Popoff however did not confess. He had come to the conclusion that even a false confession would not save him. If he was to be liquidated, he would be liquidated, confession or no. Why should he therefore present the GPU with a semblance of legality, particularly as he had survived the 'major battle' without breaking down?

On his sixth day in the Lubyanka and after a total of twenty-one interrogations he was brought before a sort of tribunal. Dzerzhinsky in person, Menzhinsky and the smooth and silky Artusov once again subjected him to a cross-fire of questioning about all the accusations made against him. Popoff stood by his statements and finally Dzerzhinsky said:

> 'We are willing to believe that you have not committed the crimes against the Soviet Union with which you were charged, but you are still our enemy. You are on the other side of the barricade, in the camp of the bourgeoisie, which we have sworn to destroy and which is equally anxious to see our downfall. Everybody knows the conclusions which we draw from this; they are quite clear and straightforward. You are lucky because we have decided that it is opportune at present to release you. You are well aware of the reason. For the rest, we very much regret that this case has arisen: a subordinate official believed that your passport was not in order. Goodbye.'

When this report by Popoff on his own case was published in 1925 many of those idealists for whom the Soviet system represented the greatest social experiment of all time preferred to regard it as a fabrication, or as the exaggerations of a journalist with a good story, or at worst, an exceptional case. Later accounts were to show that the Cheka and the GPU were merely perfecting in the early twenties the methods they were to apply at the height of the Purge, an example of which follows.

Alexander Weissberg-Cybulski, an Austrian by birth, was employed in the mid-thirties as a physicist at the Ukrainian Physics Institute in Kharkov. He was arrested at the beginning of 1937 during the purge against the 'Bukharinist right deviations' and eventually taken to NKVD headquarters at Kholodnaya Gora, on the outskirts of the city, where his interrogation was conducted by Lieutenant Reznikov. Many years later he described his experiences:[2]

> 'I have just received information about you from Lygansk. It simply makes my blood run cold. You certainly aren't what we

thought you were – a minor accomplice. Oh no! You're a master-hand at counter-revolution. Here, read that.'

I read the sheets he handed to me, and then I said calmly:

'Citizen Examiner, do you really mean that you take all this seriously or are you making fun of me?'

'Accused, I warn you against keeping up your old game. It is deadly serious. Previously we failed to recognise the connections or we should never have tolerated your attitude. Thanks to the confession of Vlach and his associates we have now revealed the whole network of counter-revolutionaries you created in the Ukraine.

'Your accomplices are now under arrest. Vlach is in prison in Lugansk, Stupin in Kiev, Lessing and Joffe are here, and the rest are either in Dnepropetrovsk or in Kharkov. All of them have confessed and all of them have implicated you. There are twenty statements which accuse you of terrorism, espionage and diversionary activities. Formerly we had only clues and suspicions; now we have all the threads in our hands. What little remains you will give us.'

'Citizen Reznikov, if this goes on much longer I shall just go off my head. All this is nothing but fantasy.'

The 'confession' put before Weissberg gave details of a terrorist organisation allegedly created by him for the assassination of Stalin and Voroshilov. In it people he had not seen for years described non-existent meetings and quoted imaginary conversations.

Reznikov and two of his subordinates took turns at interrogation. Reznikov shouted:

'Do you dare to accuse the organs of the Soviet power of having extorted false confessions! Vlach himself confesses to his crimes and yet you have the insolence to dispute them! Why should he confess things which aren't true? What is this new idea that your criminal brain has cooked up? . . .'

I was half dead. I had been sat on a stool for fourteen hours solid without being allowed to stand up and stretch my limbs. Standing up against a wall for hours and hours on end is bad enough, but sitting down is even more painful.

One of Reznikov's aides, Weissband, continued this interrogation without a pause, a technique known in prison slang as the 'Conveyor'.

'But what can I do, Citizen Weissband? I can't confess to things I have not done. Why should I deceive the Soviet power. Who would benefit by that?' In the afternoon Reznikov arrived in high good humour. 'How much longer are you going to torment us?' he asked jovially. 'We have to suffer with a bandit like you, you know. Come on now, let's have a little peace at least!'

Weissberg stood the 'Conveyor' for seven whole days. Then he was ready to give in.

> It was midnight on the seventh of my 'Conveyor'. I had fought till I dropped, but now I was beaten. There was nothing left for me but capitulation and confession. . . . Having already made my decision I hadn't to invent too much on the spur of the moment. I was to be a follower of Bukharin and to admit terrorism and counter-revolutionary organisation. On the other hand I would strenuously deny espionage and diversionary activity. One awkward point was still unsettled, and that was the problem of who had recruited me and whom I had recruited. Any confession to the GPU always began with these two questions. The answer to the first one was easy enough. I could mention plenty of likely people who were safely outside the Soviet Union. . . .
>
> The second question was much more difficult. Reznikov wanted the names of people who could be arrested by the GPU and no doubt he had my friends in the Institute in mind. . . . On this point I was determined not to budge whatever happened: I would not denounce them. During the following three hours I dictated my confession, and all the time I was wondering what to say when they demanded the names of my accomplices.

Weissberg confessed to everything that was expected from him. He concocted details of a plot to assassinate Stalin and Voroshilov and when his imagination failed him he drew upon the other confessions which he had been shown. Eventually he was sent back to his cell after a sumptuous meal to rest before continuing his confession. He was not called again until midnight the following night.

> I screwed up my courage.
>
> 'Citizen Examiner, do you really believe a word of what I signed yesterday?'
>
> At first he pretended not to understand me.
>
> 'I don't know what you mean, Alexander Semenovich. Please be a little clearer.'
>
> 'Yesterday after physical torture and after I had not been allowed to sleep for a week I made statements which were invented from beginning to end. I now consider it my duty to withdraw them completely.'
>
> 'What! You son of a bitch! You dog! You counter-revolutionary bandit! So you wanted to provoke the Soviet power? And you dare to tell me that to my face! We'll shoot you down like a mad dog.'
>
> 'Do what you like, but I was never a counter-revolutionary. I have done nothing against the Soviet power. I never organised any attempt on Stalin's life, and I have never had anything to do with

diversionary activities or espionage. The whole thing was an invention. I said it because I was physically incapable of holding out any longer. You extorted that false confession from me by illegal means.'

Weissberg was subjected to another two 'Conveyor' sessions. After each of these he again withdrew the false admissions he had been driven to make. In spite of this, he regards the 'Conveyor' as a more effective method of compulsion than direct physical torture, which came into increasing use towards the end of 1937. 'The interrogator does not have to make an effort. He can wait. Time is his ally. . . .'

In October 1937 Alexander Gorbatov, a senior Red Army officer, was arrested in the early hours of the morning. What awaited him was no different from the experiences of Georg Popoff and Alexander Weissberg-Cybulski at the hands of the Soviet Security Service. Gorbatov was later rehabilitated and distinguished himself as an Army Commander during World War II. His reminiscences were published in the Soviet Union in 1964, and later translated.[3] This is how he describes his fellow prisoners in the Lubyanka:

> They impressed me as being cultured and serious-minded people. I was all the more horrified to hear that during their interrogations every single one of them had written the most unmitigated rubbish, confessing to imaginary crimes and incriminating other people. Some had given way under physical pressure; some had been terrified merely by the threat of torture.
> This I simply could not understand. 'It is not only you and those against whom you have testified who will suffer,' I told them. 'It is your relatives and your friends. Besides, you are misleading the investigators and therefore the Soviet authorities.'

The Red Army general found it no easier than the Austrian physicist to understand the sense of extorting false confessions:

> For three days I was not called. Then, on the evening of the fourth day, I was led away to the interrogator. He checked the facts about me, told me to sit down opposite him, gave me pen and paper and said: 'Describe all the crimes you have committed.'
> 'There's nothing to write,' I replied.
> 'They all say that at first, then they think better of it. They remember and write. You've plenty of time. We're in no hurry. Those who have nothing to write are outside – free. Now you just get on and write.'

Gorbatov did not write and he did not go free. Instead, he was transferred to Lefortovo Prison and found himself in a cell with a Brigade Commander and a high official in the People's Commissariat of Trade. They both thought it better to confess immediately.

Three days passed. The sessions with the interrogator began. At first they were no different from those in the Lubyanka, but when the interrogator had convinced himself that I would not write he hissed: 'You will. They've all written for us so far, and that's the way it's going to be with you.' The fourth time I was called before one of the senior men. First he asked me quietly whether I had any idea of what I was letting myself in for. Had I thought everything out properly, taken everything into account? Then he said to my interrogator: 'Yes, I agree with you!' and left the room. . . .

Five interrogations accompanied by torture followed, with intervals of two or three days. Sometimes I had to be helped back to the cell. Then I was given a rest for about twenty days. . . .

I withstood the torture during the second bout of interrogation, but when the third bout started, how I longed to be able to die!

Once Comrade C. asked me: 'Doesn't even this convince you that you have no way out?'

'No, it doesn't,' I answered. 'I shall die if necessary, and as I die I shall repeat it – No! No!' . . .

I remember – it was the last interrogation but one – that the interrogator asked what my relations with my wife were like. I told him they were good. 'Oh, are they? Then we'll arrest her too. We can make her testify against you as well as herself.'

This is how Gorbatov describes the last day of the investigation, in May 1939:

Three men sat at a table. I noticed that the chairman wore a broad gold stripe on the sleeve of his black uniform. 'A captain, first grade,' I thought. My joyful mood did not desert me. This was all I asked for – that a court should try my case.

The proceedings lasted some four or five minutes. My surname, first name, father's name, year and place of birth were checked. Then the chairman asked: 'Why did you not admit to your crimes during the investigation?' 'I have committed no crimes. I have nothing to confess,' I answered. 'Why then do ten men who have already been convicted testify against you?' asked the chairman. . . .

I was taken out into the corridor. Two minutes passed. I was brought back into the hall and the sentence was read out: fifteen years in prison and concentration camp, and five years' deprivation of civil rights.

It was so unexpected that I fell to the floor where I stood.

The only document Gorbatov signed was, at the time of his release, an undertaking not to reveal anything concerning his case. Twenty years later, when his reminiscences were published, he wrote:

> The object of this account is to tell the younger generation about people who did not lose their faith in justice even under these conditions, their faith in our great Party and in the Soviet Power – even when many of them had lost hope of ever being at liberty again. But there were also prisoners who had abandoned all faith in what is dearest to Soviet people and whose only thought was how best to remain alive. They agreed to everything and really did become the enemies of Communism and the Soviet Nation. . . .

These few sentences from a man who experienced the worst that the regime could do say much about the tangle of loyalty, indoctrination and terror which can hold a Soviet citizen prisoner even when he is nominally free.

'Why should I deceive the Soviet power? Who would benefit by that?' Alexander Weissberg asked one of his interrogators. The answer may seem far-fetched, but it was cogent enough in terms of the Soviet regime. It hinges on the dissatisfaction which was endemic among the mass of the people. Often enough there were solid reasons for it: low salaries, a scarcity of consumer goods, high prices, a shortage of housing, harsh working conditions. If the disgruntled citizen was an orthodox Communist he might well blame the leadership for failing to solve such everyday problems under a system as perfect as Bolshevism.

The leadership was acutely conscious of this pervasive dissatisfaction, but there was nothing it could do to remove the innumerable causes of complaint. Every case taken up by the Security Service was, in this sense, a matter of chance: anyone might be suspected of disaffection and become a target for investigation. In its first stage an investigation sought to establish grounds for suspicion, in the second stage to discover other disaffected individuals in contact with the suspect. If such were found they might, then or later, form an organisation.

A false confession was therefore valuable even when the investigator knew that it was false, because it could be used to secure confessions from other suspects. These confessions, true or false, were used in the third stage of the investigation to mount cases against officials higher up in the hierarchy. For obvious reasons the case against a District Party Secretary, an Army Colonel or the Director of a large plant needed more thorough preparation than the matter of an ordinary worker, peasant or soldier who could be shot out of hand. The liquidation of a leader such as Radek, Bukharin or Kamenev naturally required special preparation for the benefit of public opinion.

'The production of a political melodrama staged in a courtroom in Moscow, Prague or Budapest needs many months of painstaking preparation just as a musical show or a motion picture, only more so,' writes Arthur Koestler in his introduction to Alexander Weissberg's *Conspiracy of Silence*. Such a production was built up from below, step by step. The confessions at the lowest level were used to topple the next higher category of officials until the summit was reached. From then on the trial acquired a reverse effect as an intimidating example.

This process was self-perpetuating as long as the machine went on working. It did so partly for very ordinary reasons, such as the professional ambition of Security officials. It used to be said in Moscow that if the slogan 'Find the enemy!' appeared in the capital, it would be 'Find the enemy quickly' when it reached Kiev, 'Find thirty enemies immediately' when it got to Kharkov. In no time at all a report would go back: 'Fifty enemies have already confessed.'

An official who secured confessions proved his efficiency and put himself in line for promotion. His colleagues who did less well might be suspected of laxity – or even of counter-revolutionary leanings. As a result, evidence continually accumulated in the Security Service archives, mostly for future use. It did not come fully into its own until Stalin had completed the most brutal stage of his rule: the liquidation of the free peasantry.

SOURCES

1. Georg Popoff, *Tscheka – Der Staat im Staate* (Frankfurt, 1925).
2. Alexander Weissberg, *The Accused* (Simon and Schuster, New York, 1951).
3. General A. Gorbatov, *Years off my Life* (W. W. Norton & Company, New York, 1965).

Part Three

THE FIRE

CHAPTER SIX

The 'Poor Peasant' Campaign

O N 14th April 1925 *Pravda* published a long article about the problems of agriculture which must have baffled many of its readers by appeals to the peasants of the following kind: 'Enrich yourselves, develop your farms, do not be afraid that restrictions will be applied against you.'

This article was an appeal to the Russian peasantry. Its message was hard to reconcile with Marxist-Leninist principles. It contained direct invitations to pursue private profit, to use agricultural labour and, by implication, to form a new privileged class. Its author was Bukharin, then one of the seven members of the Party's collective leadership. The article reversed most of what had been said and written when Lenin and his friends set up the 'Committees of Poor Peasants' in June 1918 to ensure that food was distributed fairly, by requisitioning surplus stocks of grain, and to provide agricultural machines for improved productivity on the land.

Unfortunately, such machines were virtually non-existent, while the requisitioning, brutally enforced and left to the discretion of the marauding food commandos, led to a wave of violence in the villages. Lenin had to apply the brakes within a week of launching the operation. He wrote: 'The task of the detachments for the collection of foodstuffs is to assist in collecting surpluses from the kulaks, i.e. richer peasants. It is not indiscriminate and wholesale confiscation in the course of their work.'

Regardless of orders, food collection continued to develop into mere plunder and vindictiveness directed at anyone who was a little less poor than the poorest. In August 1918 another instruction again attempted to impose order:

> The Committees of Poor Peasants must be revolutionary organisations of the whole peasantry against former landowners, kulaks, merchants and priests, and not merely organisations of the rural proletariat against the rest of the rural population.

The food situation in the towns was catastrophic. In a telephone call to Stalin at Tzaritsyn (later Stalingrad) Lenin said:

As to the food situation in Petrograd and Moscow today, there is hardly anything to be had. Things are very bad. Let me know whether you can take emergency measures as we have nowhere to turn for supplies except to you. [And a few hours later:] Send fish, meat, vegetables, in general all the foodstuffs that can be found and as much of it as possible.

Agriculture has remained an unsolved problem throughout the history of the Soviet regime. In 1964 the Soviet Union bought more grain abroad than Russia, the world's greatest agricultural producer, had exported before the Revolution.

The 'War Communism' of 1918–1921 failed to solve the problem through requisitioning and the enforced redistribution of land. Redistribution extended to the land owned by the richer peasants, the so-called kulaks. Out of over two hundred million acres owned by kulaks before 1917 about a hundred and thirty million was handed over to peasants owning small and medium-sized holdings. By 1920 there was hardly a homestead with more than twenty acres left in the country. The standard of agricultural equipment and technique of these smallholders was very low. There was one plough between two farms or more, and less than one reaper between a hundred farms. Even the few remaining richer peasants with holdings over sixty acres had to share one reaper between five holdings.

Things improved when the Civil War ended. Requisitioning stopped and demobilisation made man-power available on the land. Above all, there was a change of policy at the centre. The 'New Economic Policy' meant a retreat from Communist ideological positions. Reluctantly, it took account of the peasants' deeply rooted desire for land of their own. The country needed bread, meat and milk, and the peasants were allowed to do more or less as they liked provided they delivered the food. The regime collected foodstuffs as a form of taxation and the peasants could sell their surplus on the open market. As a result a new class of kulaks came into being. Many smallholders soon saw that their farms made no profit. They let the land to the richer peasants and went to work as agricultural labourers. The Party leadership tolerated this practice – paid labour for private employers, 'the exploitation of man by man', is anathema to Communists – because for the time being food was more important than ideology. By 1926 more than a third of all farmland, some twenty-five

million acres, had been let. Nearly 2·4 million agricultural workers
were on the payroll of the kulaks. By comparison, the socialised
sector of agriculture was negligible. At the height of the New
Economic Policy there were fifteen hundred state farms, or
Sovkhoz, employing one hundred and thirty-eight thousand
workers, and about fifteen thousand collective farms or Kolkhoz,
averaging between a hundred and twenty and two hundred acres
each, usually as a result of the merging of ten to fifteen small-
holdings.

At this stage, the 'Left' headed by Trotsky, Zinoviev and
Kamenev called for concerted pressure on the peasants while
Bukharin, the leader of the 'Right', appealed to them to seek
prosperity. Both sides advanced convincing arguments. At this
time the average annual grain production of the Soviet Union
amounted to 69·3 million tons, very little more than European
Russia had produced in 1905. In 1927 industrial production rose
by 18·2 per cent, while the agricultural output grew by a bare 4·1
per cent. The actual crop that year was two-thirds short of the
forecast. The 'Left' favoured coercion. Bukharin relied on the
profit motive. Stalin thought that the excessive and therefore
inefficient fragmentation of holdings was to blame for the shortcomings of Soviet agriculture. In September 1927 he was still
willing to back Bukharin in order to dislodge the 'Left' from the
Party leadership, but it was quite clear that Lenin's New Economic Policy had failed. In 1928 crop failures were added to the
consistently poor results in agriculture since 1923 and the grain
harvest was five million tons lower than that of the previous year.

A famine reminiscent of the worst years of the Civil War lay
ahead. Something had to be done. A degree of capitalism had
been tried on the land, and it had failed. In Bolshevik terms the
only alternative was compulsion. Mass Terror was now to be
launched against an entire section of the population.

Lenin had consistently claimed Terror as an integral part of the
Bolshevik system. The Soviet Criminal Code of 1922 gave it legal
recognition. Lenin wrote: 'The paragraph concerning Terror must
be interpreted as widely as possible, since only a revolutionary
sense of justice and a revolutionary conscience can decide under
what conditions it is to be applied in practice.' Few criminal codes
give as wide discretion to the judge as the Soviet code. All

'socially dangerous' acts are punishable and anything is 'socially dangerous' which stands in the way of socialism. Individual rights are 'granted' by the State, and can be recalled by it at any time. Under such provisions literally anything could be punished. In particular, all rights of property could be abolished if it was decided that they might hinder the growth of socialism. Class Terror was built into the system from the start.

When the Bolsheviks called for the destruction of capitalism and the annihilation of the bourgeoisie as a class, they were attacking an enemy which in fact hardly existed in Russia. At the outbreak of World War I the number of industrial workers in Russia had reached barely three million, far fewer than the equivalent number in the U.S., with a population roughly half that of Russia. The State also provided far more capital than was contributed by individual capitalists – 234,000 million roubles in 1913, for instance, which amounted to several times the investment of all the private banks put together.

Similarly, no middle class had developed comparable to that which rose in Western Europe during the second half of the nineteenth century. Below the exceedingly thin upper crust of bankers, industrialists, great merchants and higher government servants, the traders, craftsmen and lower officials were hardly better off than the proletariat. The much heralded eradication of capitalism and the middle class could bring the proletariat little profit.

In any case, the regime in its early days was badly in need of any middle-class skills available. At the start Class Terror was confined to individual cases. The struggle against the bourgeoisie so often and so loudly proclaimed by the Bolsheviks was little more than a way of distracting attention from current difficulties and providing a scapegoat.

Class Terror began in good earnest when the Soviet leadership decided to move against the peasants, the only significant category of private owners in Russia. The attack was launched in the spring of 1928 after a Plenary Meeting of the Central Committee, when there could no longer be any doubt that the current agricultural policy had failed. It took the form of three measures: a new system of taxation, increased rates of agricultural deliveries and a new agricultural labour law.

Middle-sized holdings were now taxed on a flat rate, while the larger farms were assessed individually. In both cases the taxes were set so high that they threatened the existence of individual holdings.

A vivid illustration of the new rates of delivery of agricultural produce was the Savyalovo Method, so called after a village of that name. It was simply decided that the kulaks were to provide sixty-five per cent of the 'Norm' imposed on the village, while the medium holdings provided the rest. Failure to comply involved a cash fine of five times the value of the deficiency.

The official object of these measures was to obtain hoarded grain from the kulaks. In practice, its purpose was to force the owners of large and medium sized holdings to surrender them and join a kolkhoz, or collective farm. The new Agricultural Labour Law was a further means to the same end.

Up to this point the regime had paid little attention to the welfare of agricultural labourers. Now all farmers employing paid labour were obliged to give formal contracts to their workers and register these at the Village Soviets. Village Soviets were enjoined to enforce the statutory conditions: an eight-hour day, one free day per week, obligatory insurance, monthly payments in cash. These conditions had a 'progressive' look but were wholly unworkable. Most kulaks had no alternative but to dismiss their labourers and join a kolkhoz willy-nilly, because they could not work their land unassisted. Political discrimination was applied on top of economic pressure. The peasants made up eighty-five per cent of the population of Russia at the beginning of the century. In 1917, in the only free elections ever to be held in Russia, the Social Revolution Party which had mainly a peasant following obtained twenty-one million votes out of a total electorate of thirty-six millions. The new electoral law put an end to peasant majorities: sixty industrial or office workers elected one representative to the district Soviet; it took two hundred peasants to do the same. Kulaks were regarded as exploiters and therefore debarred from voting.

The Committees of Poor Peasants were revived in order to speed up collectivisation. By the end of 1929, in fourteen of the administrative districts of the Soviet Union there were over twenty-four thousand of these committees with some two hundred and fifty thousand members, mostly agricultural labourers and peasants who had been exempted from tax. These committees obviously regarded it as their main purpose to make things difficult for the large and medium landholders. Pressure was successfully applied and there was a dramatic increase in the number of collective farms. At the end of 1927 only 2,022 kolkhozes had been started, consisting of 416,700 formerly independent holdings. In mid-1929 there were 54,045 kolkhozes comprising over a million individual holdings. By the end of October 1930 more than two million farms had been collectivised, – one-twelfth of the entire Soviet farming industry. In many areas the kolkhozes absorbed up to twenty per cent of the farms.

It very soon became apparent that this violent transformation had an adverse effect on agricultural production. The Committees of Poor Peasants went ruthlessly into action and the prisons began to fill. In 1929, for instance, seventeen thousand peasants were sentenced for various offences against the tax, grain delivery and agricultural labour regulations in the area of the Middle Volga, and thirteen thousand five hundred in the area of the Upper Volga. In the end Special Commissioners had to be sent from Moscow to empty the prisons and get the peasants back to the fields. The Party leadership itself took fright at the activities of the Committees of Poor Peasants. The Committees were promising tractors, reapers, sowing equipment and credits immediately and in unlimited quantities so as to report the highest possible figures for new entries into the collective farms. Kolkhozes founded on the strength of such promises were clearly not going to last and further deterioration in food production would inevitably follow. A commission of experts was formed in Moscow under the chairmanship of Yakovlev, the People's Commissar of Agriculture, to submit a draft law on collectivisation to the Politburo. This Commission examined the course of collectivisation in over a thousand selected areas representative of the Soviet Union as a whole. Yakovlev and his experts came to the conclusion that it would take at least five years to collectivise all agricultural land.

This investigation, completed at the end of 1929, found little favour with Stalin. In January 1930 the Politburo decided to set up a second commission in which politicians predominated over the experts in agriculture. Its chairman was Molotov, who was Stalin's choice although he lacked special knowledge of agriculture, and Yagoda, the Deputy Head of the OGPU, was one of its members. Conditions on the land grew worse even before this commission reported. Fifty thousand complaints in writing against abuses of power by local kolkhoz organisations had been received by the end of 1929, and resignations from collective farms began to accumulate.

Theoretically, entry into a kolkhoz was voluntary and resignation from it a matter of choice. On resignation a member was nominally entitled to compensation amounting to roughly half the value of his original contribution, but as the official valuation of land represented a fraction of its real price this compensation was worth between a tenth and a twentieth of the true value. The piece of land which a farmer who resigned had the right to claim was of little use to him without livestock, equipment or the means to make a fresh start. Neither the Village Soviet nor the Committee of Poor Peasants was likely to regard a deserter with favour, and a flight to the city was the only solution. In view of all this, the prevalence of mass resignations indicates how intolerable life must have been in the collective farms.

The ferment over collectivisation had spread throughout the country by the beginning of 1930. In March Stalin himself was forced to clarify his position in an article in *Pravda*, entitled 'Made Dizzy by Success', in which he reproved the overzealous. In April, a second article, 'An Answer to Comrades on the Collective Farms', tried to deal with the misgivings aroused by the earlier article. These misgivings are well illustrated by one of the countless letters of protest which were reaching Moscow at the time:

> Comrade Stalin, I am an ordinary worker and a reader of *Pravda* and I have always studied its articles carefully. Can anyone be blamed for taking notice of the outcry and the noise over collectivisation, and of the question about who is to direct the kolkhozes? All of us, the simple people and the Press, have neglected this fundamental question. Even Comrade Stalin seems to have slept the sleep of the just and neither seen nor heard our mistakes. Therefore some of the blame attaches to you as well. But now Comrade Stalin shrugs off all the blame onto the local authorities and covers himself and the leadership in this way.

The consumers soon felt the results of these excesses of zeal. During 1929 and 1930 the number of cattle fell by 14·6 million, the number of pigs by a third. The animals died, particularly in winter, through lack of fodder and attention. The new, reluctant collective farmers showed little interest in beasts that no longer belonged to them, while the members of the Committees of Poor Peasants were too busy organising things to bother much about work in the byres and fields.

In the meantime the Molotov Commission lost no time in altering the recommendations of Yakovlev's experts. The corn-growing areas on the lower Volga and in the Northern Caucasus were to be fully collectivised within two years. The remaining corn-growing areas were given two to three years, and land under other crops three to four years, to complete collectivisation. A draft decree was published on 30th January 1930, and on 1st February the Central Committee ratified 'Measures to ensure socialist reorganisation of agriculture in areas of total collectivisation and to suppress the kulaks.'

Voluntary entry into collective farms was abolished. The wealthier peasants were classified in three categories:

Rich farmers actively opposing the new order and therefore guilty of subversive counter-revolutionary activity were to be arrested and sent to forced labour. Where resistance occurred heads of families were to be shot. They were in any case immediately separated from their dependants and sent to separate labour camps.

Those kulaks who did not resist but refused to accept collectivisation were to be deported. The Molotov Commission recommended that kulaks displaying 'loyalty' should be allowed to enter collective farms, but only as agricultural labourers and initially without voting rights. They could only achieve full membership after a probationary period of three to five years.

The Central Committee rejected the recommendation about the third category of peasants on the grounds that, as a matter of principle, there could not be any 'loyal' kulaks deserving such preferential treatment.

The decision sealed the fate of some ten million kulaks, a whole social class; but even the vast Soviet security organisation was unable to enforce Class Terror on this unprecedented scale unaided. Some twenty-five thousand picked men from factories in the larger towns were mobilised in 'Workers' Brigades'. Only those were selected against whom the GPU representatives in the plants concerned had no objection. Seventy per cent of these were Party members, eight per cent belonged to the Komsomol youth organisation and the GPU representatives on the spot checked all the names. These Brigades were given a month's training before they were sent to the villages. The labour unions organised a further 180,000 brigades of five to ten men each. Local industrial undertakings also sent commandos. These workers were to fill the gap created by the deportation of the kulaks and to nip any attempt at resistance in the bud.

The People's Commissariat of Agriculture stated that the value of kulak property requisitioned and handed over to the collective farms amounted to 180 million roubles. Unofficial reports put the real value at 400 million roubles up to the summer of 1930. This was the economic result of what was claimed as a spectacular step forward by the Soviet authorities. The human consequences of the Mass Terror directed against the free peasants did not figure in the estimates.

Ten years after Stalin's death the Central Committee of the Komsomol published *Men are no Angels*, the novel of a young Soviet author.

The hero of the story, early in the thirties, is Platon Goreevich Yarchuk, a poor peasant from a village in the Ukrainian district of Vinnitsa. All his misfortunes spring from the Order of St. George which he was awarded for bravery during the defence of Port Arthur in 1905. When famine follows collectivisation he trades the Order for a sack of meal. There is no fat to be had. Yarchuk smashes his pig's trough, which now belongs to the kolkhoz, and boils the pieces to extract the residue of swill. The skimmings of the brew, together with the meal, make gruel. A man with a Tzarist award for bravery is naturally suspect. Yarchuk is arrested and accused of counter-revolutionary activities. A toy rifle made of a lilac branch is found in his house; it counts as a firearm. The GPU goes to work. Yarchuk signs whatever is put before him and is sent to prison for two years, having confessed to the formation of a subversive group.

Presently, he is told that there has been a mistake, but as some reason has to be found for his arrest he is forced to confess his crimes as a member of the collective farm. He duly admits the theft of the trough. This earns him a second, seven-year sentence, and he finds himself doing time as a metal worker on the White Sea Canal construction just as a wave of arrests hits the engineers in charge. The GPU begins to investigate everybody's background so as to discover their accomplices. Yarchuk has lost all sense of fear after the living hell which he has experienced, but his son is a trainee pilot whose career would be wrecked if the GPU traced the relationship. Yarchuk decides to stage an accident at work: suicide would inevitably attract an enquiry. But it is too late: the young airman has already been dismissed as the son of a counter-revolutionary.

The publication of *Men are no Angels* shows that by 1963 the Soviet authorities were prepared to admit past horror; but only in fiction – no official documents on the true facts of collectivisation have yet been published. There are, however, numerous reports by individuals who succeeded in escaping from the Soviet Union about conditions in the so-called resettlement areas, such as the steppes of Kirghizia:

> We live in a hut. The sun beats down mercilessly. The hut leaks everywhere when it rains and all our belongings are drenched. We sleep on the bare ground. We have no beds, tables or chairs. We work till we fall. The bedbugs keep us awake. We are made to work on the manure heap, the main form of employment here. The dung has to be mixed by hand with artificial fertiliser, even in the hottest weather. Our only salary is one kilo of black, sour flour every ten days.[1]

In 1937, Alexander Schwarz, a Volga German who reached the forest area of Vyatka with one of the first convoys of deported kulaks, described the organisation of a camp. Completion of the 'Norm', the daily quota of work from each camp inmate – nine hours of timber felling – was rewarded by 500 grammes of bread, 20 grammes of fat and 10 grammes of sugar. New arrivals traded their clothes, their shoes and even their wedding rings for food from the local peasants. When these reserves ran out the death rate shot up. According to this report the majority of deportees died within the first three years.[2]

Another report published in 1937 came from a Finn, Olaf Feldheim, who had visited the Kuznestk coal-mining area to which many kulaks were deported.

> The geological strata showed clearly on the freshly-cut rock face, fertile black loam at the top, then clay, then the coal seams. Between black trenches at the foot of many of the slopes lay what looked like dumps of rubbish. Black human shapes, adults and children, rose from these heaps. Their eyes followed us.

'What's this? Are those really people?' I asked in astonishment. My companions' reply was coarse laughter.

'Spetspereselentsy – Special Settlers,' explained our new specialist in local affairs. 'There are thousands of them, hundreds of thousands. They were brought here as volunteers, that's why they are not allowed into the camps and hutments. If one of them wants to eat he must work. If he can't work he might as well start to dig his grave. But it's all voluntary, of course. It's all up to them. So they have to live in holes in the ground. The earth is warm, you know. You dig yourself a hole, put a few boards over it if you can steal any, and that's your lodging. Work? You get that from the GPU, whatever it happens to want. The women work too. . . .'

By July 1930, 320,000 peasant families had been deported and no less than 35,000 complaints against illegal deportation had been lodged, of which only some 2,000 were declared to be valid. This was only a beginning: 1·1 million peasant families had been classified as kulaks in 1927, and when Stalin talked to Churchill about collectivisation he spread ten fingers, one finger for each million peasants deported.

The deportations were a hasty, unplanned business. Everything was improvised. In the early stages most of the deportees went to the White Sea area. Endless trains of cattle trucks guarded by special GPU units rolled towards Archangel through the depths of winter. The first arrivals were billeted in peasant houses, often several families to one room. Later, barns and byres were used. When these were full the deportees were left to their own devices and often enough had to make do with holes in the ground until they could build mud huts of their own. This was criminal waste even from the Soviet regime's own point of view, since the labour of hundreds of thousands of workers was thereby uselessly squandered.

It was intended that the deportees to the Far North should develop agriculture in these formerly barren areas to provide food for the industrial centres of the Soviet Union. In Siberia nearly a million acres of fallow land were allocated to newly created agricultural collectives, as well as some fourteen million roubles to enable each family to buy a horse, a cow, sheep, pigs and poultry.

In practice these Siberian collectives, like the other deportee settlements in thinly populated parts of the country, were simply forced labour camps. Thousands died on the way to them.

Attempts to escape usually ended in execution. In the reception areas the GPU kept up its standard of cruelty and did little else. No statistics of the cost in human life have ever been published and were probably not even available to the regime itself. The economic results, however, are plain enough. The yearly average of Soviet grain production between 1924 and 1928 amounted to 69·3 million tons; it increased to 77·4 million tons in 1936–1940. Collectivisation and the horrors of the campaign against the richer peasants resulted in an increase of 8·1 million tons of grain per year or an annual growth rate of less than one per cent.

In the last resort Mass Terror directed against a whole class of society had adverse effects on the regime which had launched it. The Soviet authorities used fear as a bulwark against disaffection and it came to take the place of common sense in everyday life. The Village Soviets and the Committees of Poor Peasants tried to collectivise as quickly and comprehensively as possible so as to avoid the appearance of laxity. The GPU tried to report as many large convoys of deportees as possible. In the areas to which the peasants were sent the efficiency of the local authorities was measured by statistical reports on resettlement. The quality of the results was of secondary importance: it was not checked, and probably could not be. Russia was large and the Politburo was a long way away. It was a matter of fulfilling the Plan, even the Terror Plan. The system was caught in its own net.

By the end of the twenties pressure on the kulaks had become Moscow's last hope of finding reserves of food and averting famine. The wealth accumulated by the kulaks would also, so it was thought, provide investment capital for the accelerated development of heavy industry. In the event, Bukharin who had described the alleged millions of tons of hoarded grain as a fairy tale was proved right; reserves of grain did not increase and liquid capital did not become available. Collectivisation failed even to cure the food shortage. Worst of all, the kulak as the oppressor of the village was replaced by the anonymous but even deadlier oppression of the kolkhoz. After 1930 there was little to distinguish a collective farmer from a Russian serf before his emancipation nearly seventy years earlier. The amount of his contribution to the collective farm was fixed by law. In 1939 the minimum contribution was 60–100 working days per year depending on local conditions. During the war the minimum rose to between

100 and 156 days. The collective farmer gradually became a full time agricultural labourer with little time to spare for his personal plot or livestock. By 1950 the average annual contribution of individual members to their collective farm had risen to 307 days for men and 192 for women in the Ukraine.

After 1933 payment for work on collective farms was made partly in cash and partly in produce. The average daily value of this payment in 1938 represented twenty-two kopeks in terms of 1914 prices. In that year landowners in the Petersburg area were paying their peasants thirty to forty kopecks per day, all food being provided free.

SOURCES
1. Lilian T. Mowrer, *Prison and Exile* (New York, 1941).
2. A. Schwarz, *In Wologdas weissen Waeldern* (Altona, 1937).

CHAPTER SEVEN

The Anti-God Campaign

A T the end of 1922 the People's Commissar of Justice, Nikolai Krylenko, acting as a prosecutor even before the trial had begun, declared:

> The fate of Citizen Tikhon is in our hands and you can rest assured that we will not spare this representative of classes of society which have oppressed the Russian people for centuries and have not to this day given up the thought of fighting against the sovereign will of the proletariat. The Soviet Government is firmly resolved to mount a counter-attack against these attempts. It will proceed mercilessly and display no indulgence.

Military expressions came easily to Krylenko since he had been promoted from Ensign to Commander-in-Chief in 1918. He added:

> The proletariat must consolidate the positions which it has won. One of the most important stages in the battle which we are conducting is the fight against religious prejudices and the blind fanaticism of the masses. We have declared war on religion, on every denomination of every kind.

Citizen Tikhon was the Patriarch of the Russian Orthodox Church to which over eighty per cent of the population of European Russia belonged. His army, the only one which the Soviet authorities had been unable to overcome, consisted of more than fifty thousand monks and nuns and some forty-five thousand secular priests.

The Patriarch Tikhon had been in prison since the latter part of 1922. His indictment included the accusation that he had hindered famine relief. This referred to events during the summer of 1921 when famine struck the thickly populated districts along the Volga. The Central Committee had 'authorised' collections in churches and 'allowed' the starving population to turn for assistance to the religious communities. Patriarch Tikhon had responded by a call to the churches to put church plate and valuables not required for religious use at the disposal of the relief authorities.

His appeal met with only moderate success. The local priests were reluctant to part with their treasures. They suspected with some justification that the valuables might well be put to uses other than famine relief. They were supported in this by many of their parishioners who did not want to part with the ornaments of the churches and regarded their sale as a profanation.

The Soviet authorities saw in this a good opportunity for the confiscation of church property, and the 'Central Fund for Assistance to the Starving Population' provided an impeccable stalking-horse. In February 1922 the Central Committee decreed the expropriation of 'all valuables of gold, silver and precious stones the loss of which would not affect the requirements of the cult concerned'. These were to be seized by special commissions and handed over to the People's Commissariat of Finance 'for the use of the Central Fund'. It was, of course, left to the discretion of the commissions to decide what was to be confiscated, and the 'requirements of the cult concerned' became much less important than the value of the objects available.

The commissions immediately met resistance which here and there turned into open revolt in the smaller and more remote localities. This brought the GPU into action. Two thousand court cases were brought against priests and laymen who had opposed confiscation. In Petrograd eighty-five people, including the Metropolitan Venyamin, were indicted and ten of them, together with the Metropolitan, were sentenced to death.

In March 1923 it was the turn of the Catholic clergy, and Archbishop Zepliak, the Head of the Catholic Church in Russia, and his deputy, Monsignor Butkevich, were also sentenced to death.

In the meantime Krylenko had prepared the trial of Patriarch Tikhon, an act of almost unbelievable audacity: for ordinary Russians the Orthodox Patriarch stood above all earthly things and seemed far more invulnerable than the Tsar had been. Events were to show that he would retain some of this invulnerability.

The fight against religion had been part of the programme of all Marxist organisations ever since Marx had described religion as the opium of the people. Lenin had enlarged on the subject:

> Religion teaches those who spend their lives labouring and in
> want to be humble and patient in their earthly existence, and assures
> them of a reward in heaven. Those on the other hand who live by

the labour of others are taught to be charitable, are offered a cheap justification of their thieving existence and are sold a pass to ever-lasting bliss at the appropriate price. . . . The fight against religion must not be limited, or restricted to abstract ideological instruction. The fight must be linked with concrete, practical class movements, and its aim must be the destruction of the social roots of religion.

Since the French Revolution, all movements seeking to over-throw the existing social order have been bitterly hostile to religious establishments. Rulers and priests have been allies, to their mutual advantage, since the dawn of history. In Tzarist Russia the Orthodox Church owned about half of the 375 million acres that were expropriated in 1917. Apart from such practical considerations the Bolsheviks were also driven to attack religion because it represented a rival faith. Communism might be a materialist movement but particularly in a country as retarded as Russia it could not do without dedication and faith. Bolshevism therefore became a religion, claiming infallibility and tolerating no rivals, the only true way to salvation. In the words of an Orthodox prelate:

A teaching emerged which offers itself as a substitute for faith in God. . . . There are Councils – Congresses at which the dogmas are proclaimed. There are dogmas and infallible authorities which it becomes a crime to doubt even to the slightest degree. There is faith in future bliss to which every present happiness must be sacrificed, and which is intended not for us but for future genera-tions. There are saints and their images on placards and portable portraits, there are Church banners, the red flags, choral singing, texts from Holy Writ, sermons, hymns, thanksgivings and con-fessions. The cult has its priests and its Olympian gods who benevo-lently accept constant songs of praise. There are inspired leaders and infallible popes whom all must obey without contradiction.[1]

The old faith had to be uprooted to make way for the new.

First, all Church land was confiscated. Next, all schools were subordinated to the State. This was followed in December 1917 by the law on Civil Marriage, and the registration of births by the State came into force.

The fury of the masses turned against the priests just as it did against landowners, officers, senior civil servants and the rich. This required no elaborate organisation, merely the unleashing of the revolutionary mob and lynch law, while the Cheka carried out death sentences.

'Madmen, come to your senses,' began the pastoral letter in which the Patriarch excommunicated the Council of People's Commissars. The latter could afford to disregard it. Even the faithful were swayed by the redistribution of land and much as they might believe in God, and honour the Patriarch and the Metropolitans, the ordinary priests, often poorly educated and immoral, commanded little respect.

As long as the Civil War lasted the Bolsheviks had enemies enough to contend with, without launching an all-out attack on the Church. As soon as the threat to the regime receded a danger appeared that the Church might strengthen its hold on the increasingly prosperous peasants.

The famine on the Volga provided the régime with a welcome excuse for the second stage of its attack on the Church. Millions who starved while the priests hoarded gold and silver made up a picture that would convince even the faithful, and the refusal to release Church property came within the scope of the law against counter-revolutionary activities.

Nikolai Krylenko's case for the prosecution against the Church was easy enough to make.

A few weeks after the Heads of the Orthodox and Catholic Church had been arrested, Muscovites were offered 'an unparalleled spectacle', as *Izvestia* put it, on 10th January 1923:

> An endless procession of gods and priests stretched out from the Sadovy Square, a visual education in thousands of years of barbarism. Everything is represented: a Buddha sitting cross-legged with hands raised in blessing; a Babylonian Mardoch and an Orthodox Mother of God; Chinese bonzes, Catholic priests and the Pope of Rome blessing his new followers from a brightly coloured automobile; a Protestant pastor on a long pole with a gown most artfully set in motion by strings. A Russian pope in typical vestments offers to marry anybody for an appropriate fee. And there goes a monk astride a coffin full of holy relics! He too offers his wares to uncritical buyers. A Jewish Cantor, arms raised, intones the parody of a hymn. . . .

This blasphemous carnival was staged by the students of Sverdlovsk University as part of the celebrations which the Komsomol – the Young Communist Organisation – arranged on Church holidays. While Krylenko prepared for the trial of the Patriarch the anti-religious propaganda machine went into top gear. Attempts were also made to find pliable priests who could control those on whom the propaganda had no effect. A so-called 'Second All-Russian Council' deposed Patriarch Tikhon on March 1923 and lifted the sentence of excommunication which he had imposed. An organisation calling itself the 'Living Church' was created to collaborate with the regime's Religious Administration. It declared that 'the Soviet authority is the only one in the whole world which fulfils the ideals of the Kingdom of God'.

It would be wrong to regard all the members of the 'Living Church' as paid agents of the State Religious Administration. Some were opportunists, some were ready to compromise in order to save whatever could still be saved. There was also a group of reformers who believed that this was the time to remedy both the reactionary views of the higher clergy and the lack of education and occasional immorality among the ordinary priests. The regime now appeared well placed to deal with the Patriarch. His much-publicised trial had been repeatedly deferred during the first half of 1923. Protests were pouring in from abroad. Suddenly the Soviet Press surprised everybody with the brief announcement that Patriarch Tikhon had been released.

The reason for this release soon became obvious. The Patriarch had signed a document dated April 1923 closely modelled on the standard form of GPU confession.

> I recognise my legal responsibility under the articles of the criminal laws set out in the indictment, according to which anti-Soviet activity is involved. I repent of these actions against the State and I ask the Supreme Court to vary the security measures taken against me, in other words, to release me from custody. At the same time I declare that I will no longer be an enemy of the Soviet Regime. . . .

This act of total submission was signed by the man who five years earlier had challenged the regime with the words, 'Madmen, come to your senses.'

There was more to come: when Tikhon died in April 1925 *Izvestia* published what amounted to his testament. In it Tikhon once more invited Orthodox believers to obey the Soviet authorities on the strength of a text from the Epistle to the Romans: 'Let every soul be subject unto the higher powers, for there is no power but of God: the powers that be are ordained of God. Whosoever therefore resisteth the power, resisteth the ordinance of God: and they that resist shall receive unto themselves damnation.'

It has never been satisfactorily explained how this testament came to be written and there is even some doubt about its authenticity. But, paradoxically, it represents an admission of failure by the Soviet authorities, because they had been forced to secure the Church's blessing as a regime ordained by God. This marks the failure of the spiritual Terror. The physical Terror against religion continued.

After Tikhon's release, eighty-four bishops and about a thousand priests were displaced for refusing to subscribe to the 'Living Church'. After Tikhon's death the three highest dignitaries of the Orthodox Church, the Metropolitans Piotr of Krutitsa, Sergi and Serafim, were deposed for refusing to conform publicly with the spirit of Tikhon's testament.

The GPU went into action again and Metropolitan Sergi capitulated after three months in prison. He was released in March 1927 and three months later reaffirmed Tikhon's text from the Epistle to the Romans in a pastoral letter.

This act of submission was opportune. Stalin was about to liquidate the kulaks. In order to prevent an alliance of the Church and the richer peasants against the regime the persecution had to be relaxed. This was none too easy to implement: years of anti-religious propaganda had left their mark on the Committees of Poor Peasants and the Village Soviets. Stalin had to intervene personally. His *Pravda* article 'Made Dizzy by Success' set out among other things to defend the village clergy: 'I am not speaking at all of those revolutionaries, if one may call them so, who start to reorganise a community by taking down the church bells. To fetch down the church bells – just think of it, what a revolutionary deed!'

The closure of village churches was forbidden in March 1930. A few weeks earlier the authorities had tacitly accepted the plea of Metropolitan Sergi that priests who tilled their own land without hired help could not be classified as kulaks. By 1932 collectivisation had been generally completed, the kulaks had gone and persecution could be resumed with a view to putting an end to the Church.

The new campaign included a sort of Five Year Plan for the League of Militant Unbelievers. All religious symbols would be abolished, and training for the priesthood ended, by 1933; all religious meeting places would be shut by 1936; and all remnants of religious activity were to be eliminated by 1937.

The State followed suit. In December 1932 all persons not gainfully employed – and priests in particular – were banned from residing in or near the larger towns and obliged to carry special passports. A decree of 1929 forbidding the communal reading of the Bible and the teaching of the Gospel to children was now applied and set off a new wave of arrests. In Krasnogorsk the discovery of a 'Bible Plot' resulted in sentences of fifteen years' forced labour for five Orthodox, three Catholic and ten Protestant clergymen. In Leningrad, the Metropolitan Iosif and two priests were executed for supporting the 'Church of the Catacombs', an active organisation of the faithful who refused to recognise the priests of the 'Living Church'.

In 1937 alone, at the peak of the anti-religious campaign, 1,100 Orthodox, 240 Catholic, 61 Protestant and 110 Muslim places of worship were closed during the year. The number of religious communities fell from 30,000 to 20,000 between 1937 and 1938. It is easy to imagine how all this would have ended if the approach of war had not forced Stalin to seek to reverse his policy once more because he needed the support of the Orthodox Church.

SOURCE
1. M. Polski, *The Canonical Position of the Senior Hierarchy in the USSR and Abroad* (Jordanville, 1949).

CHAPTER EIGHT

The Campaign of Organised Cruelty

The compartment into which I was pushed had room for four passengers. There were sixteen of us. When the door slammed, we found ourselves pressed into a single block of flesh, and once the train started, the door was not opened again during four days and a half.

So we were ferried across Russia, a solid mass of starved, thirsty, half-suffocated creatures who became something less than human. Not being able to move we were racked by terrible cramps. We slept standing and satisfied our needs standing. With every hour the atmosphere in this foul box grew more pestilential. As the train rolled on, we drifted into a state of blurred semi-consciousness in which the brain ceased to think and the senses to feel.

At Rostov the door was opened. We had a breath of air, a drink of water and a little food. First I drank, for the ordeal by thirst had been worse than the ordeal by hunger. Then I turned to the food. Each of us was given three hundred grammes of black bread and a few sprats. I tasted the sprats; they were so salty that I forced myself not to eat them. I had heard stories about prisoners on long convoys like ours who had gone mad or died from thirst from eating those salt fish before being locked up again. I did not risk the sprats and ate only the bread.

Then the door was shut on us again and the train moved on. Our taste of air, food and water had revived us and we felt the horrors of the journey more acutely until we sank back into merciful insensibility. After five more days we were unloaded in Moscow.

When we prised ourselves loose from one another and shuffled out of our box, two bodies fell to the floor. Two men were dead and must have been dead for some time. They had died on their feet, held up by our packed living bodies, and nobody had noticed it. The smell of death was not stronger than the general stench, and their immobility not strange where no one could move.[1]

EL CAMPESINO, the author of this gruelling account, was famous throughout Europe in the thirties. His real name was General Valentin Gonzalez and he had been one of the leading supporters of the Republican regime during the Spanish Civil War. After Franco's victory he fled to Moscow – and the Lubyanka. He was one among tens of thousands of left-wingers who sought asylum in the Soviet Union as one country after another fell to the Fascists, and were caught in Stalin's purges. Among them were German Communists who had fled after Hitler seized power in 1933, Austrian Schutzbuendler escaping from the Dolfuss regime, and Spanish freedom fighters.

This influx represented a much greater threat to Soviet authority than the disaffected within the country. The refugees had proved their dedication to Communism in action. They believed that they were coming home after enduring Fascist Terror and their disillusionment was bound to be correspondingly great.

The Mass Terror had reached unprecedented proportions by the time this flood of refugees reached the Soviet Union. In 1913 there were some 700 prisons in Russia designed to hold about 200,000 convicts, and with an actual population of some 170,000. By 1927 persons under sentence in prison officially numbered 198,000, excluding, of course, those held without trial by the GPU in prisons or concentration camps. A GPU official who defected to the West reported that there were 662,257 forced labourers in the camps in the mid-thirties. Other statistics quote 734,000 prisoners under GPU control as early as 1929. An official Soviet report dealing with 'genuine' as opposed to political crimes, estimated in 1927 that 'the number of persons in prison has risen annually by fifteen to twenty per cent between 1922 and 1926 and has in fact doubled in the course of these five years. For every person who has left prison on completion of sentence, three others have entered it.'

The campaign against the kulaks flooded the prisons. The documents of the Smolensk Party Headquarters, captured by the Germans during World War II, vividly illustrate the conditions prevailing at that time. Things clearly became too much even for the GPU. In February 1930 a report complained that practically everyone was arresting everyone else. Anyone connected with collectivisation acted as policeman on his own account. Another report suggests that the Committees of Poor Peasants and the Workers' Brigades brought from the towns were following the motto: 'Drink and eat – it all belongs to us!' The wave of arrests threatened to bring on anarchy. In May 1933 Stalin and Molotov issued a secret order against all those 'who wish to carry out arrests, but strictly speaking have no right to do so'.

This more or less put an end to the arbitrary exercise of private justice. Organised Mass Terror, however, went on and now acquired economic importance.

The judicial authorities of the Russian Federal Republic estimated in 1932 that the value of the forced labour in the camps of that Republic alone amounted to some 305 million roubles. Slave labour had become essential to the fulfilment of the Five Year Plan. Molotov, then Chairman of the Council of People's Commissars, declared in March 1931: 'We have never made a secret of the fact that we use the labour of healthy and able-bodied convicts to carry out certain projects. We have done so in the past, we do so today and we will continue this practice in future.'

There were at this time six main areas of labour camps in the Soviet Union: The Solovetskie Islands to the west of Archangel, the Kond and Myag Islands in the Bay of Onega, the area round Murmansk, the area of Archangel and an area near Turkestan, in the south of the Kazakh Republic. These camps first came under GUMZ, the Chief Directorate of Penal Establishments, a department of the People's Commissariat of Internal Affairs. Early in the thirties a separate department was created to run the camps belonging to the GPU. This was GULAG, the Chief Directorate of Camps, which became in time the largest employer of labour in the world. At its height, after the end of World War II, GULAG administered nearly fourteen million forced labourers spread over more than a hundred camp areas.

Some of these groups of camps became outstandingly important to the Soviet economy. The Dalstroy group in the far east served the gold mines of the Kolyma River. Another group to the north and east of Lake Baikal was engaged on the construction of the Amur railroad, while another railroad was built by the inmates of the Pechora camps between Kotlas and Vorkuta, in the extreme north of European Russia. Forced labour laid out a complete new industrial area near Archangel, including airfields, harbour installations on the White Sea, railroads and even a large new town, Molotovsk. It was here that between November 1931 and August 1933 the famous White Sea Canal was dug as a link with the Baltic. It is estimated that 300,000 convicts were employed on its construction and 72,000 of these were certainly granted amnesty at its completion. Finally, an entirely new mining area was created around Karaganda, in the Kazakh Republic.

Certain camps were reserved for particular categories of forced labour. Karaganda, for instance, was the normal destination of foreign Communists who had sought refuge in the Soviet Union and also contained a large women's camp for the wives and widows of Communist leaders who had been 'purged'. After World War II, the Vorkuta camps were used as the collecting point for soldiers under sentence for desertion and treason. At Komsomolsk, in the far east, there was a 'Traitors' Camp' for specially dangerous counter-revolutionaries and other disaffected persons. The groups of camps on the Kolyma and at the mouth of the Ienissei included camps for 'incorrigibles' who had committed acts of insubordination elsewhere. The annual mortality rate in these camps was estimated at thirty per cent. The Shido camp in the far east had a particularly sombre reputation because prisoners who attempted to escape from it were kept in chains for the remainder of their sentences.

During the winter of 1933–34 interest was aroused all over the world by the plight of 104 Soviet sailors drifting on an ice floe in the Arctic. The SS *Chelyuskin* had set out from Leningrad to Vladivostock as part of a scientific expedition to prove that a passage along the northern coast of the Soviet Union was possible even during winter. The expedition failed and the *Chelyuskin* sank in February 1934 after being caught in pack ice. The crew could only be rescued by air, but the Soviet Government declined all offers of help from Western airmen on the grounds that this was a matter of honour for the Soviet authorities. Only Soviet aircraft were allowed to fly to the Sea of Chukotsk where the ice floe was drifting although this involved delays in rescuing the crew.

It became known much later that reasons other than pride may have caused the refusal of foreign help. A new liner, the *Dzhurma* on its maiden voyage from Vladivostock to the mouth of the Kolyma River with 12,000 forced labourers on board had been caught in pack ice less than 200 miles from the crew of the *Chelyuskin*. The *Dzhurma* was severely damaged and its passengers must have tried to survive the winter on the ice.

When the *Dzhurma* finally limped into the Kolyma estuary in the summer of 1934 there was not a single prisoner left on board. According to reports nearly half of the crew had to be hospitalised for psychiatric treatment when the liner returned to its home port. It therefore seems likely that the Soviet Government refused help from abroad for the rescue of the *Chelyuskin* crew because foreign fliers would almost certainly also have found the victims of the *Dzhurma* disaster.

The White Sea route was regularly used for the transport of forced labour. An eye-witness reports on conditions in the hold of a ship carrying 7,000 convicts:

> During the entire voyage lasting one week not a single member of the guard detachment or crew visited the hold. They did not dare to do so, particularly because of the large number of murderers and bandits on board, since they represented a tiny, if heavily-armed minority in relation to the prisoners. . . .
>
> Nobody bothered about what was going on below decks. The criminals therefore instituted a regime of terror on all such voyages. If they wanted the clothes of a counter-revolutionary they simply took them. If the man concerned showed the slightest fight he was beaten up. The food was taken from the old and weak. It is no wonder that large numbers of prisoners died in each of these transports.[2]

A modern map of the Soviet Union displays the town of Magadan on the south-east coast of the Sea of Okhotsk in Siberia. Half a century ago this town did not exist. It was built by millions of forced labourers put ashore here week after week since the early thirties. Regular traffic by sea round the eastern tip of Siberia was impossible. DALSTROY, therefore, decided to build Magadan and then drive a motor road to the north through hundreds of miles of Siberian taiga to the goldfields on the Kolyma.

DALSTROY was the special administration created by the GPU at the end of 1931 to develop the Kolyma goldfields. Even today, its record reads like a piece of adventure fiction about a miracle of technology forced upon nature. The road had to be driven through a primeval forest where up to 50,000 trees might have to be cleared for every kilometre of track. The foundations for this road were deeper and more solid than anywhere else in the world because the frozen top layer of soil could turn during a thaw into a mire six feet deep. In Magadan, today a model settlement, scientific institutes collect research data towards the agricultural development of the Arctic. Crops have been planted there for many years past. Kolyma breeds varieties of vegetables and oranges are grown in hothouses. These technical achievements cost the lives of hundreds of thousands of slave workers. During what is described as the 'foundation period' of Magadan probably only one in fifty of the DALSTROY's forced labourers survived a spell of work in the Arctic forest.

Even the founder of the DALSTROY did not live to see his work completed. Reinhold Berzin, a Latvian Communist who had taken part in the 1905 Revolution and later became an officer in Lenin's famous Latvian Sharpshooter unit, was virtually the autocrat of the Magadan–Kolyma project until the autumn of 1937. His personal power and his private army of NKVD troops began to worry even Stalin. If the creation of Magadan resembles an adventure story, Berzin's end is more like a cheap thriller. The Head of DALSTROY was lured into an aircraft specially sent from Moscow by means of a forged copy of *Izvestia* announcing that he had been awarded the Order of Lenin. He was flown back to the capital and shot. Magadan, however, remained the centre of one of the most important areas of forced labour in the Soviet Union. Its gold output, – 16/18 million ounces a year – has helped to make the Soviet Union into one of the world's greatest gold-producing countries.

Another eye-witness describes conditions in the labour camps in the Siberian wastelands after the slave transports had discharged their cargo:

> Half-naked, barefoot and half-dead we came to a lonely, terrible and frost-bound spot in the tundra where a board nailed to a post read: 'Camp Site No. 228'. With superhuman efforts we dug *zemlyankas* – mud-filled holes barely covered with twigs and earth. Our food is uncooked flour mixed with water. At night, people pile on to the litter of twigs spread over the morass and huddle together for warmth. The nights are full of groans, curses, shouts and threats. Irritation grows and people come to hate each other. At four in the morning the *naryadzhik*, or overseer, calls reveille by beating on a saw with any implement that comes to hand. You don't need to dress, because you have never taken off your clothes. Breakfast consists of the rest of the flour handed out the night before, if it has not been stolen or eaten during the night. At five comes the second gong, for the *razvod* – the assembly – when tasks are distributed among the working groups. Slowly, one after another, the men, dirty and in rags, crawl out of the *zemlyankas* and form up in four ranks, half-dead, their teeth chattering with cold. But only half of the men have surfaced. The *naryadzhik* and the *lekpom*, or sanitary

assistant, go into the dormitories, stick in hand. The overseer asks the first man he sees why he has not come out. 'I am sick,' he replies. The *lekpom* feels his pulse and declares him fit. This earns the man a shower of blows and he is pushed out into the open. 'Why aren't you outside for work?' the overseer asks the next one. 'I am sick,' comes the sullen reply. The day before this man had asked for the medical assistant and given him his shirt, dirty and infested with lice. The medical assistant feels his pulse and diagnoses a high temperature. The man is excused from work. Another claims that he has neither a shirt nor shoes. 'Take those of a sick man,' is the overseer's judgment of Solomon. The sick man defends himself and his belongings are taken from him by force. If you refuse to take a sick man's clothes you are pushed out into the open, into a temperature of − 40 Degrees Fahrenheit, and the clothes are thrown out after you. . . .[3]

The forced labourers of Camp Site 228 were building a road parallel to the railway tracks. First the snow had to be shovelled away before the stunted bushes of the tundra could be cleared and levelling started. The norm, or set task, was twenty square metres a day for each prisoner. The regulations of the Ukhta-Pechora NKVD Camp indicate the standard of monthly rations per person, as soon as a camp was 'regularly organised': twelve kilogrammes of bread, four kilogrammes of fish, a little less than three-quarters of a kilogramme of meat, fifteen kilogrammes of vegetables, twenty decagrammes of sugar and twenty seven decagrammes of vegetable oil. Piece-work earned a daily bonus of 600 grammes of bread if the norm had been carried out. The ration for the guard dogs was double that of the prisoners. Even so, food bonuses for piece-work had to be paid for out of wages. The regulations stated that: 'In those cases in which the wages of the worker are insufficient to pay for additional rations, the amount of bread is to be correspondingly reduced to the amount for which the camp inmate can pay.'

Conditions in the forced labour camps undoubtedly improved over the years, particularly after the original wastelands, primeval forests and steppes had been gradually tamed:

This was roughly how a normal day developed: we were woken at four-thirty. We washed, and breakfasted at five in a canteen with tables. . . . At six we marched off to work after each brigade had paraded with its brigade leader at the front. Outside the camp, we were taken over by the 'convoys', of which there were four or five for every group of twenty prisoners. These guards were armed with automatic pistols. They only carried machine-guns when there was an unusually large number of prisoners to escort. Then we set out to the working site. At that time we were building a settlement for railway workers employed on the Murmansk line which ran past the camp. . . . Work continued till one o'clock. Then a cart arrived and soup was handed out. Afterwards work continued till six, when there was a roll call. We marched back to camp and were given supper. Then we were free to do as we liked. . . .[4]

According to official Soviet legal doctrine, the purpose of forced labour camps was 're-education', both for those who had been sentenced in the courts and for those who had been imprisoned by the GPU and its successors without trial. Great emphasis was therefore put by the authorities on 'educational work'. Another eye-witness reported:

I can say, on the strength of five years of experience, that the whole official clamour about cultural amenities of the camps is in sharp contrast with the barbarously wretched camp conditions and the low standard of living. In practice there are virtually no books in the camps, the radio is merely a means of official propaganda. It is technically very poor at all times and highly unpopular among the camp inmates. If a radio receiver breaks down in the huts most people are usually rather pleased about it and never ask for it to be repaired. Film shows are reserved for the camp aristocracy – at most a tenth of the camp population. After their twelve- to thirteen-hour stint the workers go to bed as soon as they have eaten. They are frequently woken up again during the night for additional labour. . . .[5]

One of the reasons for the improvement of conditions in the camps was that GULAG represented an increasingly important factor in the Soviet economy. The State Trust for the exploitation of slave labour had its own production norms to fulfil and an excessive rate of wastage threatened Plan fulfilment. Statistics for 1941 for instance, show that the NKVD's Chief Administrations were expected to provide 14 per cent of the building work, 12·5 per cent of timber and 2·8 per cent of coal output, 40·5 per cent of chromium production and 75 per cent of gold production for the entire Soviet Union. Apart from GULAG a number of other Chief Administrations handled forced labour, such as DALSTROY, GUSHOSDOR for highway construction and GLAVZHELDORSTROY for railroad construction.

The Chief Administrations were constantly re-organised over the years, their names and their subordination changed, but their purpose remained the exploitation of man-power in penal camps.

Regardless of the merits of their case, millions of human beings were degraded to the state of slave labourers. Among them were both real criminals and every kind of enemy of the regime, people 'purged' for good reasons or none, people duly sentenced by law and those on whom rested only the vaguest shadow of suspicion. The campaign against the kulaks was only a start. The purges launched after 1934 provided the next batch of slave labour. The largest contingent came when the Hitler-Stalin Pact of 1939 put the population of the Baltic States and later that of a part of Poland into the hands of the Soviet authorities. Class Terror became the Terror against the Nationalities. It assumed gigantic proportions after 1945 when millions of the conquered were handed over to GULAG. Statistics compiled from some 14,000 sworn statements collected after the war in the West, indicate that the average death rate in the labour camps reached twelve per cent. In other words, over twelve years the entire slave labour force perished and had to be replaced.

In the early thirties, however, the forced labour system was still in the early stages of its development. Then Stalin began to establish his personal power over the Party and the Soviet State.

SOURCES

1. Valentin Gonzalez (El Campesino), *Life and Death in Soviet Russia* (G. P. Putnam's Sons, New York, 1952).

2. Elinor Lipper, *Eleven Years in Soviet Labor Camps* (Chicago, 1951).

3. S. Mora and P. Zwerniak, *La Justice Soviétique* (Rome, 1945).

4. Anonymous, *Zwangsarbeit in der Sowjetunion* (Vienna, 1953).

5. From a Collection of Documents Submitted to the United Nations by the US Government, June 1952.

CHAPTER NINE

The Party Line Campaign

O N 25th September 1936 the Politburo received a peremptory telegram from Stalin: 'The immediate appointment of Comrade Yezhov as People's Commissar of Internal Affairs is unquestionably necessary. Yagoda is proving incapable of dealing with the Trotsky-Zinoviev Block.' Stalin went on to complain that the Security machine was at least four years in arrears 'in the struggle against the irreconcilable enemies of the people'.

It was indeed four years earlier, in 1932, that Stalin committed himself to the course which perfected what we know as Stalinism. As an exile in Mexico, Trotsky described Stalin's victory as 'the triumph of bureaucracy over the masses'. In fact, however, it was no more than Lenin's own system taken to its logical conclusion. We cannot now tell whether Lenin, if he had lived longer, would have gone the same way as Stalin. At any rate, the collective leadership remained unchanged after his death. It was embodied in the Politburo, the executive agency of the Central Committee; the Council of People's Commissars, the official Government of the Soviet Union, was merely the executive arm of the Politburo and this enabled Stalin to dominate the State as soon as he secured control of the Politburo. Between 1922 and 1941 he occupied no government post. As General Secretary of the Party he was bound by majorities at Party Congresses, in the Central Committee and in the Politburo. The Party machine which Stalin himself had perfected secured his power but limited it at the same time. In the Party, and therefore in the State, Stalin's power depended on the consent of the Politburo.

As long as the General Secretary commanded a majority in the Politburo he could be virtually certain of a majority in the Central Committee. This, in turn, as good as guaranteed an unassailable majority at Party Congresses. The delegates sent to Moscow by the local Party organisations followed the known leaders on important questions. These delegates were Party officials, and this inhibited any leanings they might have towards the democracy which undoubtedly existed in theory within the Party. If one got a bad name among 'those at the top' one did not get to the top oneself. Stalin's success rested on this acquiescence, because the Party Congress supplied a pliant Central Committee, and the Central Committee a pliant Politburo. Once this system was set in motion it continued to function until some altogether unusual event set off a revolt in the Politburo. Then and only then could the new line be passed down to the Central Committee and on to the Party Congress as the new verdict of the gods.

To secure power, therefore, those groups or individuals in the Politburo which might form a majority against the General Secretary had to be neutralised. The next move was to disable all those who might come together at lower levels in the Party to outvote either Central Committee decisions at a Party Congress or decisions by the Politburo in the Central Committee. Khrushchev in his secret speech showed how perfectly this technique was carried out at the Seventeenth Party Congress in 1934: 1,108 out of 1,966 delegates were arrested as counter-revolutionaries in the wave of purges which followed the Congress, and 96 out of 139 members and candidate-members elected to the Central Committee were liquidated.

It took Stalin ten years of preparation to set this technique in motion. One might well ask why he found it necessary to do so. An individual does not suddenly decide to become a dictator and send millions to their death, however ruthless he may be by nature, as Stalin certainly was. He was also a revolutionary, an underground fighter and a terrorist from his earliest days and could not afford a delicate conscience. No doubt these personal characteristics added to the brutality of Stalin's bid for absolute power, but they did not affect the real reason for his bid, which was his determination to save a regime driven to the verge of collapse by its economic difficulties. Stalin, always a pragmatist, sided with the right wing against the Trotsky-Zinoviev-Kamenev group as long as there was the slightest hope of obtaining foodstuffs by treating the peasants gently. As soon as it became clear, by 1927, that this hope had failed, Stalin adopted the ideas of his left-wing opponents who had just been silenced. This period ended in 1930 with the silencing of the right wing and the fall of Bukharin, Rykov and Tomsky. Stalin was now the only representative of the Old Guard elected to the Revolutionary Committee on 10th October 1917 and the only one to have been a Politburo member without a break from the start. As General Secretary he had to find a new team in 1930 to deal with the economic crisis, the threat of famine and the impending split within the Party. The economic crisis was causing the formation of splinter groups and 'fractions'; if a split developed it could easily lead to the collapse of the regime. This might have brought about real democracy in the long run, but the immediate results would have been administrative chaos, popular disturbances, even a new civil war. Stalin could have claimed with some justification that if he could save himself he would also thereby save the Soviet régime. The converse, of course, was equally true, and others knew it. The contenders for power to the right and left invariably stopped short of openly forming a fraction, because they realised that a split in the Party spelled the end for all of them.

The Politburo elected on 13th July 1930 by the Sixteenth Party Congress consisted of fifteen men. The full members were Stalin, Voroshilov, Kaganovich, Kalinin, Kirov, Kossior, Kuibyshev, Molotov, Rykov and Rudsutak. Mikoyan, Chubar, Petrovsky, Andreyev and Syrtsov were candidate-members. The job of this team was to save the regime in the worst crisis since the Civil War.

It would be difficult to exaggerate the gravity of the crisis. The Mass Terror which accompanied the campaign against the kulaks had revived the chaotic conditions of the Civil War years. Discipline had slackened. An orgy of violence and plundering was taking place. In the eyes of the peasants – and they still formed a majority of the population – the Communist Party had become a gang of murderers and looters, and all to no good purpose insofar as the Party leadership was concerned. Famine, which until now had only afflicted the cities, began to spread through the countryside as well. In 1932 and 1933 only strict food rationing averted a major catastrophe.

Conditions in industry were equally deplorable. The Five Year Plan proved a failure. Coal production fell fourteen per cent short of the planned output, iron ore thirty-eight per cent, steel forty-three per cent and cotton textiles fifty-two per cent. Tough disciplinary measures in industry achieved little, nor did the introduction of piece-work, which Marx had branded as the ultimate weapon of capitalist exploitation. In this supposedly classless society labour developed a hatred for management which would not have been out of place in any industrial country during the nineteenth century. In 1931 groups of bureaucrats were put on trial to demonstrate that sabotage and conspiracy were to be blamed for the failures of Soviet industry. The moment of truth had come for those experts who had been put to work but were not Communists. Young Party technocrats trained in the meantime were to take their place, but there were still far too few of these available. The census of 1926 registered only half a million citizens with higher educational and technical qualifications. The labour unions displayed markedly 'opportunistic' and 'trade unionist' tendencies, which the regime no longer tolerated after 1930.

The constant interference of the local Party organisations was resented in industry. These local organisations, on the other hand, also reacted against the centralising tendencies in the higher reaches of the Party. There might well be a grass roots revolt if some members of the leadership were to act as spokesmen for the discontented; the latter could only be purged from the lower rungs of the Party if the Politburo was agreed on the measures to be taken. By 1932 Stalin was forced to muster his supporters.

Rykov and Syrtsov had been excluded from the Politburo. Andreyev and Ordzhonikidze had taken their place. Rudzutak had become Chairman of the Central Committee. Stalin could only be certain of Molotov and Kaganovich among the full members of the Politburo. Voroshilov and Kalinin would side with the majority. The remainder were against any drastic purge of the Party because they feared that this would weaken the Party machine.

The balance of forces was not encouraging. Stalin set out to create a shadow government that would be completely loyal to him. Poskrebyshev was appointed as his personal Chief Secretary and Yezhov, another member of the Central Committee, moved to the Commission for Purges. Stalin secured the nomination of Vyshinsky, Rector of Moscow University, as Deputy State Prosecutor and later as First State Prosecutor. These three men owed their promotion not to the Party, but to Stalin alone.

A mass purge was still out of the question. Only a few groups who had been too loud in their criticism were eliminated in 1932 by forced exile, under relatively bearable conditions for senior officials at least. They might be needed again. In fact, Bukharin, Rykov and even members of the 'left' such as Zinoviev, Kamenev and Radek unexpectedly reappeared at the Seventeenth Party Congress in 1934 to confess their errors. This was the so-called 'Congress of the Victors' in honour of the victory proclaimed over the economic difficulties. It was the occasion for the last attempt to prevent a coalition of the discontented by allowing them to humble themselves rather than liquidating them for good. Lower down in the hierarchy the GPU had a free hand, but a member of the leadership could only be arrested if the Politburo agreed to it.

Within the Politburo a conflict was brewing between Stalin and Kirov. Kirov had been one of Stalin's own men. The General Secretary had advanced him to become leader of the Leningrad Party in the place of the fallen Zinoviev. This was a position of great power because the former capital with its large industrial resources and its revolutionary tradition provided a natural counter-weight to Moscow. Kirov was old neither in age nor as a member of the Party leadership. The younger generation of Party officials who had grown up after the Revolution could regard him as their representative. Seventeen years after the Revolution these younger men longed for quieter times. In their eyes, both the rightist and the leftists had failed. The food problem had not been solved and industrialisation was beset by difficulties. The 'Revolution in One Country' was hardly more successful than the World Revolution. The Soviet regime faced the triumph of National Socialism in Germany instead of standing before the open grave of capitalism. Stalin had got rid of the great 'Elders' – Trotsky, Bukharin, Zinoviev, Radek – and as the last of them he now carried the blame for all the mistakes and miscalculations of the past, for the famines and the breakdown of industrial plans. A new and younger man was needed to bring about more settled conditions. Kirov could have been such a man. He was murdered in his Leningrad headquarters on 1st December 1934.

Menzhinsky, Dzerzhinsky's successor as Head of the GPU (or, more correctly, OGPU) died just before Kirov. It was claimed that he had been poisoned and four years later Genrikh Yagoda was indicted for this crime. For the time being, however, Yagoda was promoted to Menzhinsky's post.

Time was running out for the OGPU. In June 1934 the Soviet Security Service was completely reorganised. The All-Union

People's Commissariat of Internal Affairs (NKVD) was revived as a central agency despite the federalist Soviet Constitution. The corresponding People's Commissariats in the Union Republics were subordinated to it, and the Russian Socialist Federative Soviet Republic, the dominant constituent part of the Soviet Union, was denied an NKVD of its own. The Russian heartland was to be policed direct by the All-Union People's Commissariat.

The OGPU, formerly an independent agency, was incorporated into the NKVD. A host of new abbreviations flooded the official Soviet vocabulary, of which the most important was probably GUGB, the Chief Administration of State Security. It was seldom used outside the inner circle of those concerned and became merged in people's minds with the NKVD as a whole. This now came to stand for the executive agencies of the Mass Terror, as the words Cheka and GPU had done in earlier days.

The GUGB took over both of the GPU's main functions: to combat counter-revolutionary activities and to dispose of the counter-revolutionaries. The latter was the responsibility of the 'Special Council', a board consisting of two senior NKVD officials and a representative of the State Prosecutor's Office. The Special Council deliberated in the absence of the accused. The NKVD official who had conducted the investigation was the chief witness. The documentary evidence usually consisted of a perfect confession. In theory the Special Council could only award a strictly limited range of sentences: expulsions from certain places or from the Soviet Union as a whole; or a spell of forced labour or deportation to a penal camp for terms not exceeding five years.

From 1937 on the Special Council also issued death sentences. In practice the NKVD took over to a large extent the functions of the regular courts. Apart from genuinely criminal cases, only cases likely to provide spectacular propaganda effects reached the courts. A new political crime was also introduced during this period – family guilt by association. The relatives of suspected and convicted persons were described by the abbreviation TshIR.

In practice the principles once laid down for the Cheka remained in force and the reorganisation was merely a matter of centralising and tightening up the security machine. The reorganisation was timely in view of the tasks that would presently confront the NKVD. The Great Purge was launched on the day after Kirov's death. On the very night of the murder the General Secretary issued a strict instruction to all Party and Government agencies concerned that political cases were to be prosecuted with the utmost urgency and death sentences carried out without delay, regardless of petitions for clemency. The Politburo was left to ratify this personal instruction by Stalin retrospectively.

The first trial was staged on 30th December. Kirov's murderer, Nikolaev, and thirteen alleged accomplices were sentenced to death and shot. This otherwise insignificant event was important because the Leningrad group of conspirators could be represented as supporters of Zinoviev. This was the starting point needed for the liquidation of the entire opposition within the Party, from minor provincial officials to former members of the Politburo.

Were the proceedings against the lower and middle officials in the Party launched to establish the existence of a conspiracy, thereby incriminating the star personalities? Or were the show trials of men who had long since lost every vestige of power staged so as to justify a massive purge of the rank and file? In fact, these motives complemented each other. The leaders were liquidated because they might become rallying-points for the discontented, and also to show very clearly that nobody should feel safe, even if he had shared a room with Lenin in October 1917. The rank and file were liquidated to prevent the formation of opposition groups. Present innocence and actual crime were immaterial in these terms. All that mattered was possible future conspiracy. This threw a shadow on anyone who held the slightest degree of authority in the Party or in the management of the economy. Prevention was the keynote and as practically everybody in the Soviet Union had some grounds for grumbling, the sweep of the Terror was limited only by the resources available to the NKVD.

Within the Party the first wave of purges, which occupied the whole of 1935, was carried out through the Party's own organisation. Stalin filled the key posts with men on whom he could absolutely rely. Yezhov was promoted to Head of the Party Control Commission. Another young man in Stalin's Secretariat, Georgi Malenkov, became his closest collaborator. Andrei Zhdanov succeeded Kirov in Leningrad. Nikita Khrushchev headed the Moscow Party as First Secretary. As a result, the purge proceeded without a hitch. The Party withdrew its protection from the suspects and the NKVD was able to operate freely.

Thousands, maybe tens of thousands, of lower and middle rank Party officials went to forced labour camps by way of the interrogation cells and the Special Council.

Two years earlier the Politburo had been doubtfully loyal to Stalin and might have outvoted him in certain circumstances. Now it remained silent. It accepted Stalin's arbitrary acts and even legalised them retrospectively. The shock of Kirov's murder hardly provides a sufficient reason for this acquiescence. Admittedly, further cases of sudden death followed that of Kirov, such as that of Kuibyshev in January 1935. Two years later a baffled Soviet public was informed that Kuibyshev had been poisoned by Yagoda, the Head of the GUGB. Whatever may be the truth, the case conveyed the awful warning that nobody's life was now safe.

Another death soon followed to point the lesson. Maxim Gorky was the poet of the Soviet regime, a writer and a personality above all reproach, on a par with Lenin. Early in 1935 his work began to be subjected to ill-founded criticism in the Soviet Union clearly licensed from above. Then Gorky died, in June 1936; in the following year his death was also blamed on Yagoda and poison.

Today all this reads like an Elizabethan melodrama about the palace intrigues in some provincial capital of Renaissance Italy, where a false monk mixes poison with the sacraments. No wonder that many Western democrats, who saw in the Soviet Union a regime founded on noble and humanitarian doctrines, refused to believe that Stalin and his supporters could sink as low as the crimes with which they charged their victims. These well-wishers of the Soviet State even rejected the suggestion that the Government of one of the greatest countries in the world sent innocent men to their deaths on the strength of false confessions. Those Soviet leaders who might have put a stop to Stalin's growing power, however, well knew the true state of affairs.

The Terror had exactly the same meaning for those who were being purged as for those who purged them. Mass arrests, deportations, executions were perfectly acceptable practices in so far as the fallen leaders were concerned, at any rate until they themselves became the victims. Whatever their political shading, those who opposed Stalin within the Party thought in the same terms as he did, though perhaps not on the same scale.

It may be that Kuibyshev tried to halt Stalin's attack on potential dissidents in the Party machine and therefore had to die. It is also possible that Gorky had to die because he had attempted to exert his influence against the purges. But Mass Terror, the extortion of confessions and the killing of opponents presented no ethical problem for the Soviet leadership: they were a technique of Government, of expediency and efficiency. It is, therefore, not surprising that the Politburo knuckled under to Stalin.

On 25th November 1936 *Pravda*, the official organ of the Party, described the General Secretary, Comrade Stalin, as 'The Genius of the New World, the wisest man of the era, the great leader of Communism'. Two months earlier the trial of a group of his opponents had begun in the October Hall of the Trade Union Building in Moscow, specially fitted out for the occasion. The Military Board of the Supreme Court of the USSR was composed of three judges and two substitutes, with Ulrich, a Military Judge, in the Chair. The prosecution was conducted by the General State Prosecutor, Andrei Vyshinsky. Everything was done to ensure that the rules of Soviet legal procedure followed to the letter.

The sixteen defendants included two of the leading Left Deviationists of the late twenties, Zinoviev and Kamenev. The four main articles of the indictment read as follows:

1. That during the period from 1932 to 1936 a joint Trotskyist-Zinovievist Centre was organised in Moscow which set itself the task of carrying out a number of acts of terror against the leaders of the Communist Party of the Soviet Union (Bolsheviks) in order to arrogate power to itself;

2. That the following among those held responsible as accused in the present case belonged to this joint Trotskyist-Zinovievist Centre: as Zinovievists, Zinoviev, Kamenev, Evdokimov, Bakaev; and as Trotskyists, Smirnov, Ter-Vagyan and Mrachkovsky;

3. That the Joint Trotskyist-Zinovievists Centre organised during this period a number of terrorist groups and prepared a number of practical measures for the assassination of Comrades Stalin, Voroshilov, Zhdanov, Kaganovich, Kirov, Kossior, Ordzhonikidze and Postyshev;

4. That one of these terrorist groups, which were operating under the direct instructions of Zinoviev and Trotsky as well as those of the Joint Trotskyist-Zinovievist Centre and under the personal leadership of the accused Bakaev, perpetrated the despicable murder of Comrade S. M. Kirov. . . .

'I demand,' said Vyshinsky at the end of a speech for the prose-cution which had lasted several hours, 'that these dogs who have gone mad should all be shot'.

The official account of the trial takes up 185 pages. Its most striking feature is the eagerness with which the accused confessed to whatever was put to them. The only exception was Smirnov, a member of the Russian Social-Democratic Party since 1899, a friend of Trotsky's and a member of the Revolutionary Military Council after the October Revolution.

A passage from the very lengthy questioning of Smirnov by Vyshinsky is typical of the entire trial:

VYSHINSKY Did you have direct communication with Trotsky?
SMIRNOV   I had two addresses.
VYSHINSKY I am asking you whether you had communication.
SMIRNOV   I had two addresses . . .
VYSHINSKY Will you answer – was there communication?
SMIRNOV   If the existence of two addresses represents com-
           munication . . .
VYSHINSKY And what would you call it?
SMIRNOV   I said that I had received two addresses.
VYSHINSKY Did you have personal communication?
SMIRNOV   I did not have personal communication.
VYSHINSKY Was there postal communication with Trotsky?
SMIRNOV   There was once.
VYSHINSKY And did you receive a letter from Desov or Trotsky
           through Gaven?
SMIRNOV   Gaven handed over a letter from Trotsky.
VYSHINSKY I just asked you about this – whether you had com-
           munication with Trotsky, yes or no?
SMIRNOV   I am saying that I wrote a letter to Trotsky and received
           a reply from him.
VYSHINSKY Is that communication or is it not?
SMIRNOV   It is a communication.
VYSHINSKY So there was communication?
SMIRNOV   Yes.

One must bear in mind that throughout this long trial the Prosecutor was dealing not with petty criminals or subordinate officials, but with the intellectual élite of Bolshevism. These were outstandingly able, highly educated men with decades of training in dialectic argument. Presumably, the usual methods were applied during the preliminary investigation: the 'Conveyor' interrogation on a hard bench, without sleep, without rest, without food for days on end. But in the court room, and before a world audience, Vyshinsky could rely only on his own experience and ability to connect proven facts with trumped-up conclusions in order to build a convincing case. This had to be done so well that the accused could not retract their confessions, even if they wished to do so. Another example taken from Smirnov's evidence illustrates Vyshinsky's technique:

VYSHINSKY	This Directive contained a direct suggestion that it was necessary to go over to a terrorist struggle against the Party leadership?
SMIRNOV	Absolutely right.
VYSHINSKY	Against whom, in the first place?
SMIRNOV	No names were stated in it.
VYSHINSKY	But you did understand that the terrorist struggle should be undertaken first and foremost against Comrade Stalin?
SMIRNOV	Yes, that is how I understood it.
VYSHINSKY	And this is how you passed it on to those who shared your opinions?
SMIRNOV	Yes. I passed on these directives to the Centre, the Centre accepted them, but I took no further part in this work.
VYSHINSKY	When did you then resign from the Centre?
SMIRNOV	I never thought of resigning from the Centre, there was nothing there that one could have resigned from.
VYSHINSKY	The Centre existed?
SMIRNOV	But what a Centre! . . .

Smirnov's last reply is enlightening. As the months and the years went by, Stalin's opponents must certainly have spent many nights discussing what could be done about a General Secretary who was becoming a despot. Under any democratic regime this would have been a thoroughly legitimate thing to do, and only a dictator who identified himself with the State could regard such conversations as high treason. No doubt the opposition also considered the use of violence. All those concerned had reached and retained their positions through violence. Theirs was a regime that maintained itself by violence and therefore could only be removed by violence. It would have been logical for any of the accused to have said about Stalin: 'The best thing would be to kill him,' but under any normal legal system a thought is not a crime and only deeds are actionable.

It is questionable whether the Centre, which was clearly no more than a circle of Stalin's opponents, ever took any action, however trivial, apart from thinking and talking in a disaffected way. The managers of the trial relied on ready-made confessions by less important suspects to supply proof that the accused had passed from talk to action. In Smirnov's case Vyshinsky brought Citizen Safanova to the witness stand. She said:

> Mrachkovsky, who had just returned from one of Stalin's receptions, told us about a conversation with Stalin. I was present and so was I. N. Smirnov. Mrachkovsky, in telling us about his conversation with Stalin, declared that the only way out was to murder Stalin. I. N. Smirnov energetically supported this conclusion by Mrachkovsky. . . .
> Before my departure in December 1932 for construction work on the Amur–Baikal Railroad I discussed with Smirnov the future activity of the organisation in connection with the resolution adopted concerning Terror. I. N. Smirnov confirmed in categorical terms that Stalin must be murdered, that Stalin would be murdered. . . .

The first point to note in the testimony of this witness is her reference to her departure for construction work on the Amur–Baikal Railroad. This was clearly a woman who had been sent to forced labour in one of the Eastern Siberian camps. She might well have been glad of any chance to escape from this purgatory and been willing to make any statement required of her, but even she could only report what the accused had said, not what they had done.

Could the witness be believed? Vyshinsky neatly disposed of this point in the examination of Smirnov:

VYSHINSKY What was your relationship with Safanova?
SMIRNOV Good.
VYSHINSKY No more than that?
SMIRNOV We were very close to each other.
VYSHINSKY Were you husband and wife?
SMIRNOV Yes.
VYSHINSKY There were no personal differences between you?
SMIRNOV No.

What could be more convincing? Smirnov's own wife, with whom he had been on excellent terms, accused him of murderous thoughts. This instance gives one a glimpse of the full horror of the NKVD technique. The wife of a suspect is seized, forced to confess, deported to a forced labour camp and finally brought back as a prosecution witness against her own husband, thereby helping Vyshinsky to conclude his speech for the prosecution as follows:

> During the preceding days of the trial these gentlemen have attempted to assume a noble posture. They, or at least their leaders, have spoken, not without posturing, of their terrorist conspiracy; they have tried to secure recognition of the political nature of their crimes, and expected to be given it; they have talked about a political struggle, about some political agreements with some supposed political parties – liars and clowns, miserable pygmies, lapdogs and yappers who have turned against the elephant, that is all that this company amounts to!

On 23rd August 1936 all the accused were sentenced to be shot.

A month after the end of the trial Stalin went to the Crimea for a long spell of leave. He was accompanied by his closest confidant of the moment, Andrei Zhkanov. While resting he despatched to the Politburo his famous telegram requesting the appointment of Yezhov as People's Commissar of Internal Affairs and stating that Yagoda and the OGPU were proving incapable of carrying out their work. There has been much speculation as to what prompted this telegram. Had there been some hitch in the Zinoviev-Kamenev trial which outside observers had missed? Was it a matter of preparing the next trial more thoroughly? Or did a plan already exist to eliminate Yagoda himself as an inconvenient witness, possibly in connection with the cases of poisoning?

Whatever the answer, the Politburo complied without a murmur. Times had changed since 1932 when Stalin still had to worry about finding a majority to support him. Now he could issue orders by telegram while on leave. On 27th November *Pravda* announced changes in the Security Service: not only Yagoda, but six of his deputies, all of them old revolutionaries from Dzerzhinsky's days, were replaced. They were succeeded by men bought over by Yezhov from the Party's administration. This change foreshadowed the next trials and purges: it was the Old Guard's turn for the slaughterhouse and their comrades might well not be tough enough to deal with them. It might be possible to convince oneself of the existence of a Trotskyist-Zinovievist conspiracy, particularly if one had been trained as a terrorist, but what was now planned passed all bounds of credibility.

On 23rd January 1937 a further trial, again presided over by Ulrich, began against seventeen men. Chief among them were

Karl Radek, a Pole and close companion of Lenin, and Yuri Pyatakov, one of the 'left-wingers' who had protested with Trotsky during the late twenties against the neglect of Soviet industry. In his opening speech Vyshinsky went into far greater details about the activities of the accused than he had done in the earlier trial:

> Pyatakov persuaded his henchmen of the need to organise explosions and diversionary activities, preferably resulting in casualties. Drobnis asked for clarification: 'The more victims, the better,' was the answer in so far as the Trotskyists were concerned. Livshits, Knyazev and Turok organised railroad accidents. Radek dealt with foreign policy with the object of throwing the cause of socialism off the rails (just as Livshits and Knyazev had derailed trains), and of opening the gate to the foreign enemy, an enemy ever ready to attack. Here they all are before you, those who have waded in this morass of crime and blood. Consider these groups one by one: they were intimately linked with foreign spies who had bought them with promise of support or simply with ready cash. . . .

This went further than the prosecution in the first Show Trial: the accused were now alleged to be agents of foreign interests. Taking only the case of Radek, the suggestion that this indefatigable agent of the Comintern, whose whole life had been devoted to the Revolution, was a capitalist spy would have been too much for experienced veterans of the Cheka. Yezhov's new men were needed to prove the indictment.

The course of the second trial outwardly followed that of the first. The accused confessed as required. Pyatakov's testimony illustrates the loss of dignity and the revolting sanctimoniousness involved:

> Yes, I did once make the attempt to turn away from Trotskyism. This was in the years between 1928 and 1930, and I did not follow this attempt through. I have not rid myself of the remains of my past; the poisonous sting of the vestiges of Trotskyism was left within me. It was a sting which at first was of no great consequence to me, but later a malignant abscess formed around it and set me on the path of crime and treason. This abscess has now been cut open. Do not think, Citizen Judge – I may be a criminal, but I am also a man – that during these years, the years of poisonous Trotskyist illegal activity, I did not see what was going on in this country. Do not think that I had not understood what was happening in industry. . . .
>
> I did not merely understand what was happening. I also understood, although this does not in the slightest diminish the despicable

nature of my crime or its objective importance, I also understood that we, the small Trotskyist groups, the vanguard of Fascist counter-revolution as the State Prosecutor has correctly described us, could not alter by one iota the objective course of the development of the Soviet industry and economy by our spoiling activities. . . .

Further confessions built on similar foundations covered acts of sabotage ranging from an explosion in a mine caused by fire-damp to the derailment of trains. Such accidents certainly occurred and the art of the NKVD interrogators consisted in turning them into acts of sabotage and putting the blame on the accused. The fact, for instance, that an accident had happened in the Far East further suggested to the prosecution that Knyazev had acted on the orders of the Japanese Secret Service. Thirteen of the accused, including Pyatakov, were sentenced to be shot. Four, including Radek, were given prison sentences, and have not been heard of since.

The Show Trial of 1937 put an end to the opposition on the left. The turn of the rightists came in March 1938 with the trial of twenty-one men, the chief among them being Bukharin, Rykov and Yagoda. At this trial the prosecution abandoned all attempt at credibility:

> In 1932–1933 the accused, acting on the instructions of the espionage services of countries hostile to the USSR named in the indictment, formed a group of conspirators under the name of 'Block of the Rightists and Trotskyists' which set itself the following aims: espionage in favour of foreign countries, sabotage, diversionary acts, acts of terror, undermining the labour force of the USSR, provoking a military attack by these countries against the USSR, defeat of the USSR, dismemberment of the USSR and secession of the Ukraine, Belorussia, the Central Asian Republics, Georgia, Armenia, Azerbaidzhan and the Far Eastern coastal areas (the Primorie) in favour of the above-mentioned foreign States, finally, the overthrow of the social and State structure existing in the USSR, and the re-establishment of capitalism and the power of the bourgeoisie in the USSR. . . .
>
> The Block of the Rightists and Trotskyists has organised a number of terrorist acts against the leaders of the CPSU(B) and the Soviet Union and carried out terrorist acts against S. M. Kirov, V. R. Menzhinsky, V. V. Kuibyshev, A. M. Gorky. . . .

Bukharin had been co-editor of *Pravda* with Lenin, a member of the Politburo, Chairman of the Comintern and one of the authors of the Soviet Constitution. Rykov had been a member of the Politburo, a People's Commissar of Internal Affairs and then, as Chairman of the Council of People's Commissars, Head of the Soviet Government until 1930. The suggestion that these men had become spies in the pay of a foreign power and traitors bent on dismembering the Soviet Union verged on the grotesque – yet both confessed to these crimes.

Yagoda had been a senior member of the Cheka since 1924. He had twice been People's Commissar of Internal Affairs and, for two years, Head of the GPU. The evidence for the first Show Trial was prepared by his subordinates. He was now accused, over and above his other crimes, of being a poisoner. And he too confessed.

In Yagoda's case it seems that truth and fiction are inextricably mixed. It is not unlikely that Menzhinsky, Kuibyshev and Gorky were poisoned, and Kirov was certainly shot. Khrushchev in his secret speech to the Twentieth Party Congress left no doubt about the fact that Stalin instigated Kirov's murder. At the trial of 1938 Vyshinsky painstakingly traced back to Yagoda responsibility for the repeated failure to hold Kirov's assassin, but he did not indicate the source of Yagoda's orders to act as he did. Neither did Yagoda, although he too confessed in full.

In speculating about the reasons which prompted all the accused at the Show Trials to make these highly improbable confessions it is sufficient to remember that every one of these men was a dedicated Communist. Whatever their talents, their faults and the political labels attached to them, not one of them would have contemplated the destruction of the Soviet regime. Some of them may indeed have intended to murder Stalin, but only to save Socialism as they understood it. In a book published shortly before World War II called *I was Stalin's Agent* Krivitsky describes how an NKVD official induced one of the accused at the second Show Trial, Mrachkovsky, to confess: 'I brought him to the point where he burst into tears. I wept with him when we came to the conclusion that all was lost, that there was neither hope nor faith left, that nothing remained to be done except to prevent a futile rising of the discontented masses. It was for this reason that the Government needed the public confessions of members of the opposition.'[1]

The international situation of the period must also be taken into account. The Spanish Civil War had just begun when the first Show Trial was held in 1936. By 1938 and the third Show Trial Franco's victory was no longer in doubt. Communism had suffered a major political and military defeat. The Western Democracies feebly stood by while a Fascist regime established itself in Spain, Mussolini conquered Abyssinia and a vulnerable regime paved the way for National-Socialism in Austria. The Austrian State ceased to exist on 12th March 1938, the very day on which sentence was passed on Bukharin, Rykov and Yagoda. Great Britain and France made no move to save it.

Both Western Democracy and the World Revolution were in full retreat. The Soviet Union was isolated and must sooner or later be attacked. To those accused in the Show Trials and to countless other victims of the purges it was a spiritual as well as a national home. Many of them had sacrificed everything to it in the past. It embodied their dreams of the future. Regardless of Stalin and his aberrations it came first, and if it stood in danger their lives and personal integrity were forfeit to it.

One cannot tell how many confessed to non-existent crimes as a result of this spiritual and moral pressure. Only a few among the victims of the purges were brought to open trial, and the reasons for their admissions in court can only be a matter for conjecture in each case. Tens of thousands of others during the *Yezhovchina*, as this period of the great purge is called in Russia, went on their way through the NKVD interrogations and Special Councils without publicity of any kind. The scale of this wave of Terror will only be known when the NKVD archives are opened. Khrushchev's speech at the Twentieth Party Congress gave no more than a sketchy outline of it. All that we know for certain is that when the *Yezhovchina* was over only Stalin was left of those who had sat in Lenin's Politburo.

The fourth and most eventful stage of the *Yezhovchina* remains shrouded in even greater mystery right up to the present day.

SOURCE
1. Walter A. Krivitsky, *In Stalin's Secret Service* (Harper & Row, New York, 1939).

CHAPTER TEN

The Civilian Campaign

IT was Dr. Beneš, the Head of the Czechoslovak Government in exile, who in a conversation with Churchill in 1944 first outlined the origins of the Red Army purge which became known as the 'Tukhachevsky Affair'. Beneš was President of Czechoslovakia in 1935 when Hitler pressed it for a guarantee of neutrality in the eventuality of a Franco-German conflict. The request was urgently repeated late in 1936 and the Germans indicated that Czechoslovakia had better not count on Soviet help, as 'events' were impending in that country.

Beneš instructed the Czechoslovak police to investigate and was informed that contacts between members of Russian opposition groups and the German Secret Service had taken place through the Soviet Embassy in Prague. The Soviet Union was the only effective guarantor of Czechoslovak independence, France being weak, and Beneš felt obliged to inform Stalin of the reports he had received. As it turned out, neither Beneš in 1936 nor Churchill in 1944 were fully aware of the real circumstances of the Tukhachevsky Affair.

In 1936 Marshal Tukhachevsky was Chief of Staff of the Red Army and, at the age of forty-three, undoubtedly its ablest officer. His father was a wealthy landowner. As a young Guards officer during World War I Tukhachevsky was for four years a prisoner of war in Germany, but escaped in time to join the Red Army in the spring of 1918. He served as a Political Commissar rather than as a regular officer and by the end of that year already commanded an army. His further career was meteoric – it largely fell to him to turn the force that Trotsky had created to fight the Civil War into a peacetime army. One of the greatest problems was the re-establishment of military discipline and the exclusion of civilian Political Commissars from purely military affairs.

These Political Commissars were directly subordinate to a central department known as PUR, to which they had direct access without reference to the commanders of the units to which they were attached. Trotsky had been forced to abandon his dream of a proletarian Pretorian Guard and persuaded his fellow leaders in the Party to employ former Tzarist officers in the same way in which bourgeois experts were employed in civil life. But these officers were not trusted and PUR was created as the Military Section of the Central Committee to act as a supervisory agency, with the Political Commissars as its watchdogs.

By 1928 Tukhachevsky, as a Chief of the General Staff who was also regarded as politically most reliable, succeeded in removing the influence of Political Commissars from the military field at the higher levels of command. Corps Commanders were no longer hemmed in by political interference, but every one of them was a Party member. In the lower echelons, although the overwhelming majority of recruits still came from a peasant background, the élite troops were drawn as far as possible from the industrial proletariat. In the case of armoured units and motorised infantry it was officially laid down that half the strength should consist of proletarians. At this stage, thirty-seven per cent of military personnel belonged to the Party or to the Komsomol youth organisation.

The Red Army kept out of the internal Party struggle over the correct economic course to follow, and neither Stalin nor his opponents attempted to embroil it in the dispute. It nevertheless was an important, though passive factor in the struggle for power. Stalin was well aware that he could not hope to rule the country if he antagonised the army, while his opponents realised that any open revolt must fail if the army remained loyal. This enabled the Red Army to grow and develop relatively unaffected by the purges.

When the crisis came, Marshal Voroshilov was a member of the Politburo and People's Commissar of Defence. He was Head of the military establishment and assisted by the General Staff, but it was clear that most of the senior officers looked on Tukhachevsky as their real chief.

Tukhachevsky represented the Soviet Union in London at the funeral of George V in 1936 and created an excellent impression. He was due to return for the Coronation of George VI in May 1937 but it was announced that he would be unable to attend owing to illness. Soon afterwards he was demoted to command the Volga Military District, one of the least important in the Soviet Union. Then the Soviet Press revealed that a Fascist military conspiracy had been discovered and that Marshal Tukhachevsky was among those arrested.

The Soviet public was past being surprised by this sort of news. If men like Zinoviev, Kamenev and Radek had turned out to be spies, saboteurs and traitors, why should Tukhachevsky not have become a Fascist conspirator? The attitude of many officers is illustrated by the reminiscences of General Gorbatov, himself later arrested as one of the conspirators:

> I was thunderstruck by the news. I asked myself how it could happen that men who had played such a great part in smashing foreign intervention and counter-revolution within the country could have become an enemy of the people. After considering all the possible explanations, I fell back on that which was most generally accepted at the time – 'You cannot get away from class origin'. This explanation was founded on the fact that Tukhachevsky and several other generals arrested at the same time came from rich families and had served as officers in the Tzarist Army. As many said then: 'They must have got caught in the nets of foreign secret services during journeys abroad undertaken for health reasons or on duty. . . .'[1]

Trotsky himself remarked during the Civil War that Tukhachevsky was a soldier of the Revolution, not a revolutionary. General Gorbator only had occasion to revise his opinion when he, a peasant's son who had never travelled abroad, found himself in prison.

President Beneš told Churchill about the origins of the Tukhachevsky Affair in all good faith. He was wholly unaware of the facts subsequently revealed by former members of the German Secret Service, according to which the idea of discrediting the senior officers of the Red Army came from Reinhard Heydrich, the Head of the Reich Security Office. With the help of Admiral Canaris, Chief of the Abwehr, a file of fifteen documents was forged dealing with supposed secret negotiations between Marshal Tukhachevsky and the German High Command. Tukhachevsky was represented as the leader of a military conspiracy which intended to overthrow the Soviet regime, seize power and institute a new policy, more favourable to Germany. In order to add credibility to the forgery, a document was included in which Hitler ordered a close watch over Tukhachevsky's German contacts, as though Hitler was reckoning with the possibility that the German High Command might be tempted to imitate the Russian conspirators and to get rid of their own dictator.

The whole forgery was based on a history of genuine collaboration between Germany and the Soviet Union after the end of World War I. 'Special Group R' was set up in the German Ministry of the Reichswehr in the early twenties to establish relations with the Soviet Union. The initiative came from the Chief of the Army Command, General von Seeckt. Germany had been forbidden to rearm under the Treaty of Versailles, while Russia lacked the technical know-how to create an armaments industry. As a result of collaboration between Germany and the Soviet Union, aircraft, artillery ammunition and poison gas were to be manufactured on Soviet territory. This agreement petered out towards the end of the twenties, but its memory lingered and the Germans guessed that Stalin might well regard reports of treason by his senior officers as a continuation of the Seeckt contacts. The documents were allowed to fall into the hands of the Czechoslovak police, and in June 1937 Tukhachevsky, together with a number of senior Red Army officers, was sentenced to be shot after a secret trial.

One may wonder whether Stalin believed the evidence submitted to him. It certainly cannot have been entirely unwelcome, since it gave him the opportunity to disable the only force in the country that could still threaten his position. The Tukhachevsky Affair allowed him to rid the military establishment of men who had acquired far too large a measure of independence. Over 30,000 officers, half of the Red Army's strength, were purged and Political Commissars were brought back in May 1937, even before the Terror struck.

Both parties in the Tukhachevsky Affair thus achieved their aims. Stalin was able to carry out his purge and the German High Command induced its potential opponent to weaken his defences. The 'Beheading of the Army', as it became known, soon showed its results. The inglorious performance of the Red Army during the Finnish winter campaign of 1939 and the disastrous Soviet losses in the first phase of the German onslaught in 1941 are both directly attributable to the total disorganisation of the Soviet military machine after the purge of the officers.

SOURCE
1. Gorbatov, *op. cit.*

Part Four

THE WORLD CONFLAGRATION

CHAPTER ELEVEN

The Seed of Violence

IN April 1937, ten months after the Spanish Civil War had broken out, the leadership of the Spanish Communist Party met to decide whether the Communists should withdraw their support from Largo Caballero, the Socialist Prime Minister, and thereby bring down the Government. The meeting was stormy because it involved a clash of radically opposite views, and difficult because some of those taking part knew very little Spanish. Present, in addition to the Spanish leaders, were André Marty, a Frenchman, Palmiro Togliatti, an Italian, Ernö Gerö, a Hungarian, and Vittorio Codovilla, an Argentine; other participants were Stepanov, a Bulgarian, the Soviet diplomats Gaikin and Marchenko and a man known as Alexander Orlov who had directed the Transport Administration of the NKVD before coming to Spain.

Togliatti demanded the fall of Caballero. The Spaniards were silent, except for José Diaz who enquired angrily why Spanish Communists should always do whatever Moscow wanted. Stepanov quietly pointed out that it was history, not Moscow, which had rejected Caballero on account of his failures and his defeatism. Marty nodded, whereupon Diaz turned on the Frenchman and shouted at him that he was a mere bureaucrat.

'I am a revolutionary,' growled Marty.

'So are we all,' spat back Diaz.

'That remains to be seen,' retorted Marty, now thoroughly riled.

The Russians sat through it all in stony silence. They could have told Diaz why the Spanish Communist Party must take orders from Moscow: in Spring 1937, out of the 400 aircraft at the disposal of the Republican Government, Russia had supplied 200 fighters, 150 bombers and most of the remaining reconnaissance aircraft.

Caballero was duly brought down and Juan Negrin became Prime Minister. The decision had been taken by a handful of men from a dozen foreign countries, 'fairly' enough, as it did not affect Spain alone but World Revolution as a whole. It was a matter for the Comintern.

The Comintern, or more accurately the Third International, was founded in March 1919 in Moscow to unite all the militant revolutionary Marxists of the world. The First – Socialist – International had split in 1914 when the overwhelming majority of parliamentary Socialist parties backed the war effort in each country at the outbreak of World War I. The more uncompromising Marxists – thirty-eight delegates from eleven countries – met in September 1914 at the small Swiss resort of Zimmerwald, voted for uncompromising pacifism and founded the Second International. Lenin was present, but as usual he advocated a line of his own: the conversion of the Imperialist struggle into a civil war.

Circumstances favoured Lenin and proved him right. Less than two months after the Bolsheviks seized power, in December 1917, the Council of People's Commissars issued Decree No. 112 signed by Lenin and Trotsky:

> Taking into account that the Soviet regime is based on the principles of the international solidarity of the proletariat and the brotherhood of the workers of all countries, and that the struggle for peace, as well as the fight against imperialism, offer a hope of final victory only in an international framework, the Council of People's Commissars considers it necessary to support the left internationalist wing of the Workers' Movement in all countries by all possible means, including financial ones, regardless of whether these countries are waging war against Russia, are its allies or remain neutral. To this end, the Council of People's Commissars resolves to put at the disposal of the foreign missions of the Commissariat for Foreign Affairs two million roubles for the requirements of the internationalist movement. . . .

It is a remarkable document, considering its date. Lenin was thinking in terms of world revolution even though the Council of People's Commissars with its very tenuous hold on power might easily be swept away by the next wave of upheavals in Russia. Despite appearances, however, Lenin's attitude was perfectly logical: he did not consider that socialism in one country was viable, even though Stalin later tried to prove the contrary from his writings.

In the long run, Communism could not survive if Russia was surrounded by capitalist countries. World Revolution must be brought on, even though two million roubles was all that could be spared for the purpose at the moment.

Fifteen months later, the situation had radically altered. The war was over, the Central European Powers had collapsed, there was social unrest everywhere and the Soviet regime was consolidating its hold. Such Communist Parties as had come into existence by that time united in March 1919 to found the Third Communist International – Comintern for short.

From then on the Comintern became the agency for the promotion of the World Revolution. Yet its role was changing, right from the time when it was founded. As the prospects for a World Revolution diminished, so it increasingly became an instrument of Soviet foreign policy and adopted the outlook and methods of the Soviet régime, including the use of Terror to achieve its aims. In 1940, Benjamin Hilton, one of the founders of the Communist Party in the United States, a member of its Central Committee and of the Praesidium of the Comintern, stated that every member of the Comintern was briefed by the GPU before travelling abroad. If he was not a regular GPU agent, his activity came under close GPU supervision. According to Hilton, the special section of the Comintern dealing with travel arrangements and financial support for foreign Communist Parties and publications was entirely subordinate to the GPU.

By 1919, the time of the birth of the Comintern, the first and perhaps best chance for the World Revolution had already come and gone. The Central Powers had collapsed, but the imperialist conflict did not turn into a civil war. In Germany the last Chancellor of the Imperial Reich handed over in most orderly fashion to the leader of the Social Democratic Party. One of the first actions of the latter was to call Imperial General Headquarters on the telephone to make certain that the Army would prevent any rising. The Spartakist revolt was put down. A special commando of regular troops arrested Karl Liebknecht and Rosa Luxemburg, who had just founded the German Communist Party, and executed them without trial. General elections held in January 1919 gave an overwhelming majority to parties favouring a parliamentary democracy.

In Austria, the Communist Party, which had been founded only a few days before the proclamation of the Republic, fared even worse. A few flags were torn down, a few pamphlets calling for the establishment of a Socialist Republic of Workers', Soldiers' and Peasants' Councils were handed out, and that was all. At the first elections in February 1919 the Communists did not win a single seat.

The Comintern could reckon at the start on the support of some two million Party members, but three-quarters of these were in Russia. Apart from them, the only sizeable force was the Party in Germany, with 390,000 members. Nor did the prospects for the World Revolution improve as time went by: Bela Kuhn's regime in Hungary lasted barely five months, until August 1919; the Soviet Republic in Bavaria petered out after one month; and the 'Red Army' organised in the industrial Ruhr area of Germany was quickly swept away by the Reichswehr. The first assault had failed. It was now the task of the Comintern to make the world ripe for revolution.

The men engaged on this stupendous task deserve closer study. The record of their conspiratoral activities is often scrappy, but brief biographies of a few of the leaders give an indication of the quality of the rest.

Karl Radek, a Pole by birth, had chosen Russia as his home. In November 1918 he entered Germany illegally to promote the foundation of a Communist Party. He was arrested in February 1919 and only succeeded in getting back to Moscow in the following December. He reappeared in Berlin in 1922 when he was Secretary of the Comintern, a post he retained until Stalin got rid of him.

Bela Kuhn recruited the first Hungarian activists as a prisoner of war in Russia in 1916. He returned to Budapest in November 1918, arranged a merger between the Social Democratic Party and the Communists, proclaimed a Soviet Republic in March 1919 but was forced to flee in August when Rumanian troops invaded Hungary. He was back in Moscow in 1920, but was arrested in Vienna in 1928.

Ferenc Münnich's career closely followed that of Bela Kuhn in Russia and Hungary. Later, he fought in the Spanish Civil War until 1939, served in the Red Army during World War II and returned to Hungary in 1945 where he eventually became Prime Minister.

Ernö Gerö, another Hungarian, reached the Soviet Union in

1924. He later operated on behalf of the Comintern in Paris under the name of Singer and, as Pedro, organised the Catalan Communists during the Spanish Civil War. In World War II one of his duties in the Soviet Union was to supervise the publications of the Free German National Committee recruited from German prisoners of war. He returned to Hungary with Münnich and became Secretary of the Hungarian Communist Party shortly before the Revolution of October 1956.

Josip Broz, better known as Tito, was another Austro-Hungarian prisoner of war in Russia. He went back to Yugoslavia in 1920, landed in jail for organising the illegal workers' movement there, returned to work in the Balkan Secretariat of the Comintern in Moscow, appeared in Paris with a forged passport in 1936 to organise the transport of volunteers to Spain and later was again in Moscow before leading the Yugoslav partisans to victory against the Germans in World War II.

Palmiro Togliatti joined the Praesidium of the Comintern from Italy in 1926. From 1936 he acted as the senior Communist adviser in Spain until the end of the Civil War. He was back in Moscow between 1940 and 1944, when he left for Italy to lead the Communist Party.

The Russian Michael Borodin was one of the most colourful figures among the senior members of the Comintern. Lenin sent him to Mexico, the United States and Britain in 1918. He handed John Reed Lenin's 'Letter to the Workers of America' for publication. He was deported from Glasgow in 1922, then went to China in 1923 where he remained as adviser to Dr. Sun-Yat-Sen and the Kuomintang until 1927.

John Reed reached Russia from the United States in 1917, witnessed the October Revolution from the Smolny Institute, and described his experiences in his famous book *Ten Days that Shook the World*. He took part in 1919 in the foundation of the Communist Party in the United States and eventually returned to Moscow to work in the Executive Committee of the Comintern until his death.

Even these few scattered details give some idea of the world-wide scope of the Comintern's activities and indicate how every strand of its network led back to Moscow. Whatever the origin of these men and their ultimate fate, they were all trained in the school of the Russian Revolution and appeared at any point on the globe where some event demanded the presence of a leading Communist. They took on any assignment which the Party required, however different it might be from anything they had previously done. Mata Zalka, another Hungarian and a writer, taken prisoner by the Russians as an Austrian officer in 1916, was commanding a Red Army Regiment in 1920. After leading a unit of Cheka troops he became Director of the Moscow Theatre of the Revolution, later worked as one of the Secretaries of the Central Committee of the Communist Party of the Soviet Union and finished as he had begun, commanding the 12th International Brigade in Spain under the name of General Lukacs.

The great training camp of the International Brigade at Albacete during the Spanish Civil War looks in retrospect like a cross-section of Communist politics after the end of World War II. The Inspector-General was Luigi Longo, the present leader of the Italian Communist Party. Klement Gottwald, later Prime Minister and President of Czechoslovakia, was Political Adviser. The unit organised to select German volunteers and test their political reliability was headed by Walter Ulbricht who now leads the German Democratic Republic. Meantime, far away in Paris, Josip Broz, alias Tito, supplied passports and rail tickets to volunteers bound for Albacete.

The fall of the Spanish Monarchy was the result of an election in which republican, but non-Marxist, parties secured a heavy majority. The Civil War followed an attempt by right-wing Generals to seize power from the Republican Government. In spite of this initial absence of Communist inspiration the Civil War in Spain was the largest, last and most open intervention by the Comintern. Its earlier attempts to promote revolution had not been as whole-hearted, and they had failed more quickly.

The Comintern, undeterred by the failure of the attempted Communist revolution in Germany in 1919–20, tried again in 1923. A distinguished Red Army Commander, Jan Bersin, the victor of Grodno during the Soviet-Polish War of 1920, was despatched to Germany under the name of General Gorev. For several months he turned up wherever industrial trouble was brewing. The situation was favourable for a working-class rising: the French had occupied the industrial district of the Ruhr on the grounds that the German Government was falling behind with its deliveries of war reparations. The Government, supported by the Labour Unions, called for passive resistance. Work stopped in the Ruhr, acts of sabotage were countered by the French with mass arrests and serious clashes followed. Meanwhile, sporadic labour unrest occurred elsewhere in Germany.

Gorev's aim was to fuse all these isolated cases of unrest into a single countrywide rising towards the end of 1923. An even more ambitious idea lay behind this plan: the rising was to provoke a war between France and Germany; this was to turn into civil war, in accordance with Lenin's precepts, and lead to a Communist seizure of power. Gorev's attempt failed, mainly because part of the German Communist leadership refused to back him, either through patriotism or because it feared that the resulting bloodbath would not bring about a proletarian victory. Gorev was arrested and later exchanged for three German citizens held in the Soviet Union. Strikes and riots were put down by the police and the Reichswehr, to which the German Government had handed over executive powers. At the end of the year the Communist Party was banned.

This Comintern failure in 1923 played a part in the power struggle within the Soviet Union. Trotsky and Zinoviev reproached Stalin with his lax attitude towards World Revolution and the feeble support given to the German insurrectionary movement, while the General Secretary branded his opponents on the left as 'adventurists'.

The second major failure of the Comintern occurred in China in 1927. A series of risings led and inspired by Communists were bloodily suppressed. The Kuomintang Party, which united a variety of nationalist groups but strongly inclined to the left, changed direction towards the right. A whole army of Soviet military and economic advisers, including Borodin, were forced to leave China. The Communist Party itself split, the first occasion on which the young Mao Tse-Tung clashed over points of ideology with the line laid down from Moscow.

Nineteen-twenty-seven proved to be the turning-point in the policy of the Comintern. The promotion of Terror through unrest and risings was abandoned in favour of long-range diplomacy. Working-class unity now became the aim and this involved attempts to organise joint labour action with Socialists and Social-Democrats which later developed into the Popular Front movement for joint action against Fascism by all political parties opposed to it, including even middle-class liberal ones. The underlying intention remained to capture key positions within the Popular Front and eventually eliminate the non-Communist elements in it. The Spanish Civil War provided the clearest illustration of this technique.

When Lenin devised his own version of Marxism at the turn of the century he put violence at the base of all planning – since violence was clearly essential to enable a minority to achieve power and terror to maintain it there. The army of professional revolutionaries would carry out the plan. Lenin was thinking in terms of Russia where only rebellion conceived on military and conspiratorial lines could succeed, because the absence of legal parliamentary parties and labour unions precluded the creation of a mass movement. Lenin's opponents, and particularly those outside Russia, rejected his conception because they were thinking in terms of Western democracy. In October 1917 he demonstrated the correctness, if not the moral justification, of his model of socialism as far as Russia was concerned.

The problem facing the Comintern from its earliest days was how to apply Leninism to a completely different set of circumstances. The Communist Parties belonging to the Comintern usually contended with adverse circumstances because they were forced to compete in Europe and the United States with well-organised Workers' Parties and independent labour unions operating in reasonable freedom. Things might be different in Africa, Asia and Latin America, but in Europe the practical objectives of the Bolsheviks in the social and economic field could be achieved by the established Workers' Parties without resorting to violence. The new Communist Parties had therefore little or no prospect of achieving power by parliamentary means. Must these Parties also regard violence as the only means of achieving power? Did they also have to be conceived from the start as organisations of professional revolutionaries? And did their members necessarily regard themselves as belonging to a terrorist organisation, and behave accordingly?

The rank and file of Communist Parties in the twenties and thirties certainly did not think of themselves in this light. They were concerned about better pay and a higher standard of living;

the traditional Labour Parties were clearly unable to give them what they demanded; economic crises and the growth of Fascism drove them to adopt Communism. Their Communism was no more than an extreme left-wing form of Socialism: it did not imply the adoption of a radically different political, social and economic system. At the same time, the image of the Soviet Union as the fatherland of the workers, the land of dreams come true, appealed powerfully to their imagination. Whoever spoke against it must be a liar.

The politically educated leaders of the Western Communist Parties saw things in a different light, but they faced a dilemma. Moscow was virtually their only source of support and funds, yet the Comintern was dominated by rigidly Leninist bureaucrats who saw the world at large from an exclusively Russian point of view. As far as they were concerned there was only one, ready-made form of Communism and any suggestion that local or national circumstances must be taken into account made no sense to them. Anyone who suggested that general directives should be modified in the light of such circumstances was held to infringe the Party line. As a result, minor conflicts constantly occurred between the Centre and the Parties on the spot, but never a major rebellion. The Comintern's arm was too long and too powerful. In the Soviet Union this power resided in the Terror, the ability to annihilate dissenters not only socially and morally but also physically. Abroad it consisted in excommunication – let him who doubts be damned and rejected!

To enter the Communist Party during the inter-war period meant resigning one's place in Western society, especially in so far as intellectuals were concerned. A Communist aroused the worst suspicions among members of the middle class. A convert to Communism might feel in the forefront of the battle for a better world, but to his former friends, his colleagues and his relatives he almost invariably became an outcast. The Party took the place of country and family, the Party received him, but it demanded all his time and all his devotion. If he left, he lost everything, including his ideals; he continued to bear the mark of the Party and his former world might well not be willing to take him back.

This is one of the reasons why so many intellectuals shied away from breaking with the Party despite their growing disillusionment, and why they blinded themselves with the argument that however faulty or even vicious the practice of Communism might be, its theory remained perfect. Eminent men such as Arthur Koestler, Ignazio Silone, Alfred Kantorowicz, André Gide, Richard Wright and many others who broke with Communism speak of the pangs of conscience and the inner struggles they had to undergo for years before they abandoned a god who had failed them long ago.

One example will do for all these cases, that of André Gide, who wrote in 1932:

> My conversion has a religious quality. My whole being, all my senses and desires are directed to a single object; every thought, even of the most involuntary kind, leads me to it. It seems to me that the Soviet Union points the way to redemption from the lamentable state of the world today. Everything confirms me in this conviction. The most pathetic arguments of my opponents cannot sway me, they fill me with indignation. . . .[1]

Four years later, after seeing Stalin's Soviet Union for himself, Gide wrote in a different vein:

> One must see things as they are, not as one pictures them to oneself in wishful dreams. The Soviet Union has disappointed our fondest hopes, it has shown us how an honest revolution can be buried under treacherous sands. The same old capitalist society has re-established itself, a new, dreadful despotism oppresses humanity and exploits it, the whole low, despicable mentality which is typical of the relationship between the slave owner and the slave has been reborn. Like Demophon, Russia failed to become a God; it has surrendered and must now lie for ever on its Soviet bed of coals.

One further motive kept many disillusioned Communists faithful to the Party even though they recognised that it was founded on violence and Terror: Fascism, National-Socialism, and Militarism appeared to them the greater evil, a more direct threat to freedom. Russia was far away and it was different. What was happening in Russia was dreadful, but perhaps it was not as dreadful as it sometimes appeared to be. Perhaps it was merely the result of over-hasty developments in a country which had lagged by a couple of centuries behind the rest of Europe. Communism in Europe need not bring forth a GPU and could not deport ten million kulaks. It was Hitler's Terror and his threat to annihilate countless millions that Europe must fear above all.

The Western Powers were too intent on preserving peace at any price to stop him. Only the Soviet Union had the power and the will to do it. The thousands or hundreds of thousands who argued in this way ignored two facts which were about to be unmistakably brought home to them: the Comintern was now only an instrument of Soviet foreign policy; and Soviet Terror was for export.

The slogan was: 'Spain must become the grave of Fascism in Europe.' Seldom has a civil war been so well documented in literary reminiscences and novels, such as Hemingway's *For Whom the Bell Tolls* to name only the most famous. Spain attracted the radical intellectuals of the world. Foreign volunteers flocked to the aid of the Republican Government.

The revolt which the Generals had been preparing for many months broke out on 17th July 1936 after the murder of the monarchist leader Calvo Sotelo. Political passions had been building up for years and now exploded in an orgy of uncontrolled violence. Unspeakable atrocities were committed by both sides and the military picture was confused from the start.

The rest of the world was drawn into the conflict on its second day, when the Spanish Prime Minister, José Giral, sent an appeal to the French Socialist Premier, Leon Blum, for arms and aircraft. On the same day an envoy of General Franco flew to Italy and was received by Mussolini on 22nd July. Franco's request for help reached Hitler at the same moment. Mussolini agreed to send aircraft to Spain on 25th July, Hitler decided to support Franco on the following day.

The Comintern did not meet in Moscow until 21st July and then adjourned for another meeting in Prague on the 26th without coming to a decision whether to support the Spanish Government. For Stalin this clearly depended on the answer to two questions: Would intervention in Spain benefit Soviet foreign policy? Could a victory over Franco and Fascism be made to appear as victory of Spanish Communism?

When Spain became a republic in 1931 the Spanish Communist Party was tiny and doubtfully reliable from Moscow's point of view. Extreme radicalism was represented in Spain by a strong and well-organised Anarchist movement which rejected the State and all forms of State interference; advocated a society in which classes, professional interests and workers' organisations would regulate the life of the community by means of voluntary contracts and numbered some two million supporters, mainly in the industrial areas of Catalonia. Another strong political group, the Trotskyist POUM, also drew its main strength from Catalonia.

The Communist Party membership, on the other hand, only reached 3,000 three years after the proclamation of the Republic. The two advisers sent to it by the Comintern, the Bulgarian Stepanov and the Argentine Codovilla, experienced constant difficulties in restraining the anarchistic leanings which existed even among the Party leadership. By the time of the elections which preceded the outbreak of the Civil War, membership of the Party had grown to more than 10,000, but even so the Communists only secured 17 seats out of a total of 497 and represented a small minority in the Popular Front which held 278 seats in Parliament. It was extremely doubtful whether this small force with its constant tendency to deviate to the left could serve the interests of Moscow as the ostensible standard-bearer against Fascism, and it was not in the Soviet Union's interest to promote the victory of a Socialist, Anarchist or Trotskyist popular movement.

In spite of these misgivings about helping the cause of the proletariat at the possible expense of Soviet interests, the Comintern allocated one thousand million French francs to the Spanish cause. The aircraft, arms and munitions so urgently needed by the Spanish Government were not mentioned, but an advance party of Comintern representatives appeared on the scene led by Togliatti, Duclos and Gerö. Headquarters for Comintern support to Spain were set up in Paris under a German, Willy Münzenberg.

Meanwhile, Moscow remained silent. Soviet foreign policy was in a difficult position owing to the military threat presented by Nazi Germany. Only France could act as a counterweight to Germany, and France would be more or less neutralised by three Fascist neighbours if Franco won. On the other hand, a Communist victory in Spain would frighten the French middle class and strengthen the anti-Soviet right-wing political parties. Stalin decided to temporise. On 23rd August the Soviet Union signed the International Non-Intervention Protocol. A Soviet Government official decree prohibited the supply of arms and munitions to the contending sides.

Unofficially, General Krivitsky who controlled a network of

Soviet secret agents from The Hague began to organise a transport organisation for war materials.

Meanwhile a turning-point had been reached in Spain. After a series of military defeats Largo Caballero formed a new popular Front Government in which first the Anarchists and then the Communists refused to take part. Collaboration with bourgeois and liberals seemed unthinkable to people such as Diaz, Hernandez and Dolores Ibarruri. Their Comintern advisers, however, disagreed. The Communists changed their minds and entered the Government. They also began to take over the Army. Under their influence Political Commissars, most of them Communists, were attached to military units to keep an eye on the officers, whom the troops suspected, not without some justification, of pro-Franco leanings. A Russian operating under the name of Miguel Martinez looked after the training of the Commissars. Soviet representatives and agents continued to arrive in Spain, but accompanied neither by troops nor military supplies.

In September the French Communist leader Maurice Thorez at last succeeded in speaking to Stalin and from that moment things began to change rapidly. Even so there was a considerable delay before Soviet aid began to arrive in Spain. Before it did so, the Spanish Government agreed to ship its gold reserves to Russia. Towards the end of October a cargo worth 1·5 thousand million pesetas left Cartagena for Odessa. Two weeks earlier, ships carrying aircraft, guns, tanks, ammunition and vehicles set out in the opposite direction. At the same time the formation of the International Brigades began.

A whole cycle of legends surrounds the International Brigades, their bravery, their successes and the many starry-eyed volunteers who had never seen a weapon in their lives but soon became hardened veterans. These volunteers were by no means all Communists and the Brigades, contrary to popular belief, were not a private army created to establish Communism in Spain. Most of the foreigners would have indignantly rejected such a suggestion, at any rate at the start of their service. They came to fight Fascism in the open, as it could not be fought in Germany and in Italy. But a concerted attempt by the Communists to capture power step by step is nevertheless one of the clearest features of the Spanish Civil War. The Communist leadership used every opportunity and every method available to achieve their object, including the systematic use of Terror. Terror came into the pressure applied to the Spanish Communist leaders by their Soviet advisers and by the Communists to the other members of the Popular Front. Every opportunity was taken to out-manœuvre and intimidate non-Communists. The methods of the NKVD were introduced and dissenters liquidated more and more frequently. Worst of all, there were occasions when loyal troops were allowed to perish on the battlefield because a defeat happened to suit Communist plans for a take-over at that stage of the war.

The dedication and discipline of the Communist in battle, as well as the ineptitude of many non-Communist politicians, helped the Communists towards their aim. When Franco's troops closely threatened Madrid in November 1936, the Government fled but the Communists stayed. General Miaja, who commanded the defence of the capital, remarked: 'I like the Communists because they are determined. The Socialists talk, then act. If the Communists talk at all, they do so after they have acted.'

The first object of the Communist drive for power was to merge with the Socialists into a single party, thereby bringing a majority of the Spanish workers under Communist control. The Socialist leadership, and Largo Caballero in particular, knew the full value of Soviet military assistance but also understood that such a merger would mean the end of democratic Socialism in Spain. Caballero was therefore brought down at Togliatti's insistence in April 1937, despite the objections of Diaz and Hernandez. The occasion for his fall was a conflict with the Anarchists who ruled Barcelona. An internal civil war developed in the city between the Communists, supported by the police on one side, and the Anarchists, together with the Trotskyist POUM, on the other. One hundred were killed and over a thousand wounded in fighting lasting several days. The Communists demanded that the POUM should be dissolved. Caballero refused to ban a fraternal Workers' Party, however misguided it might be, and the Communists left the Government.

Communist tactics were particularly cynical in the social field; for instance they opposed a series of important measures put forward by the Anarchists and the POUM and made it clear that they would themselves promote a great scheme of reform, but only when they had secured appropriate weight in the Government, in other words when they had forced through their merger with the Socialists.

Juan Negrin, who succeeded Caballero, disappointed them. He dissolved the POUM but refused the merger. Political Commissars were abolished. The flow of volunteers dwindled to a trickle, partly because reports by earlier volunteers about the political in-fighting in Spain began to reach the general public abroad. On the international plane both the major backers of the Spanish conflict, Hitler and Stalin, no longer seemed to want victory for the sides which they supported, but merely a prolongation of the struggle. Stalin was content to let Germany embroil herself in Spain, while Hitler welcomed the growing embarrassment of the Western Powers over the conflict.

On the military front the battle for the small town of Teruel, which lasted from December 1937 to February 1938, became inextricably tangled with the political strife on the Republican side. Prieto, the Minister of War, held back the International Brigades until it was too late, because he wished to claim a purely Spanish victory. General Gonzalez – 'El Campesino' – blamed the Russians for the defeat because General Grigorovich, who used the name of Stern, had held up supplies of ammunition in order to blacken Prieto's reputation. The Communists conducted a campaign against the Minister of War, while the Socialist leadership claimed that 'our comrades are being murdered at the front because they refuse to obey the orders of the Communist Party'.

In Barcelona and elsewhere in the civilian areas the Communists intensified the Terror. In Barcelona, for instance, they took over the Military Investigation Service and turned it into a sort of NKVD. Anti-Communists were tortured and shot without trial. The Government was aware of what was going on but was too weak to intervene.

By 1938 Spain and its Communist Party had become a mere stake of Soviet foreign policy. While Communists within the country intensified their drive for complete control and General Lister ordered the troops to shoot any officers who gave the order to retreat, Stepanov informed the Spanish Communist leadership on behalf of the Comintern that they must leave the Government. Stalin was seeking an alliance with France and Britain against Hitler and a Communist-ruled Spain might easily scare off both his prospective partners.

The end came quickly. France and Britain capitulated before the Fascist dictators in September 1938 at Munich. Stalin, always a realist, understood that there could be no hope of assistance from the Western Powers against Hitler for some time to come. He therefore dropped the Republican regime in Spain as a first step towards a *rapprochement* with Germany. In November the last units of the International Brigades left the country which according to the earlier slogan was to be 'the grave of Fascism'. On 31st March 1939 Franco's troops occupied the last Republican-held towns. Three weeks later the Soviet Ambassador in Berlin called at the German Ministry of Foreign Affairs, allegedly in connection with some otherwise unimportant economic discussions. This proved to be the first of the cautious contacts that eventually led in August to the conclusion of the German-Soviet Non-Aggression Pact. The Comintern was not involved in the matter; it had exported Communism and the Terror to Spain as long as this served the interests of Soviet foreign policy. Now Stalin was about to open up a larger and more fruitful field for his exports.

SOURCE

1. Extracts from André Gide's writings on Russia are quoted from *The God that Failed* (Harper & Row, New York, 1950).

CHAPTER TWELVE

The Harvest of Violence

At the first Party Congress held openly by the Bolsheviks on Russian soil, in April 1917, Stalin presented a report on 'the problem of nationalities'. His thesis was that every nationality incorporated in the Russian State against its will – the Poles and Finns, for example – had the right to secede and found its own national State. A number of other leaders strongly opposed this thesis, among them Zinoviev, Kamenev, Bukharin, Pyatakov and Rykov – the list reads like the roll of those indicted at the Show Trials some twenty years later. Lenin and the majority supported Stalin and branded those who disagreed as 'opportunist capitulators' and 'national chauvinists'.

For the time being the debate was purely theoretical: the Provisional Government was still in power and firmly intended to maintain the integrity of the Russian Empire despite military defeats. Eight months later the Provisional Government had been swept away and the new Council of People's Commissars proclaimed the right of self-determination of all nationalities on 2nd November 1917. The 'national chauvinists', including Dzerzhinsky, the future Head of the Cheka, still opposed the measure, because they regarded self-determination as mere pandering to the petit-bourgeois nationalism of small ethnic groups; they clearly had their doubts about Lenin's claim that the Soviet State, as a paradise on earth for workers and peasants, would exert a magnetic attraction on all non-Russian nationalities. Stalin's policy was implemented in spite of their opposition. In December 1917 the independence of Finland was recognised and that of Estonia, Latvia and Lithuania followed during the course of 1918.

Twenty-one years later, on 23rd August 1939, Stalin was present when the German Minister of Foreign Affairs, Joachim von Ribbentrop, and the Soviet People's Commissar of Foreign Affairs, Vyacheslav Molotov, signed a secret protocol, the two first articles of which follow:

1. In the case of territorial and political changes in the areas belonging to the Baltic States (Finland, Estonia, Latvia, Lithuania) the northern frontier of Lithuania will represent the frontier between the spheres of interest of Germany and the USSR. The interest of Lithuania in the area of Vilna is hereby recognised.

2. In the case of territorial and political changes in the areas belonging to the Polish State the frontiers of the spheres of interest of Germany and the USSR will be broadly marked by the line of the Narew, Vistula and San Rivers. . . .

This secret protocol involved the carving up of four independent states with a total population of nearly thirty million. It was soon put into practice. World War II began on 1st September 1939 and on 17th September, when the defeated Polish Government fled to Rumania, Soviet troops moved into the area of Poland lying east of the Vistula. Stalin was retrieving what he had been willing to abandon two decades earlier and he collected his share of German plunder without firing a shot. On 28th September a territorial adjustment was agreed whereby the Soviet Union exchanged its newly conquered area between the Vistula and the Bug against the inclusion of Lithuania in its 'sphere of influence'.

It was now a matter of taking up the option on the Baltic States and at first things did not go too smoothly for the Soviet Union. She demanded the right to maintain military bases in all four countries. Finland refused. When Soviet troops moved against her on 30th November 1939 the tiny Finnish Army held back the vastly superior Soviet forces for nearly three months, an inglorious episode which showed up the weaknesses resulting from the purge of officers that followed the Tukhachevsky Affair. In March, however, Finland was forced to surrender the Vyborg Isthmus and parts of Eastern Karelia. The other Baltic States complied with Soviet demands for bases in June 1940 and were incorporated into the Soviet Union a few weeks later as Socialist Soviet Republics.

After the end of the Civil War Stalin had demonstrated in his native Georgia and elsewhere that his practice in matters of nationalities differed sharply from the theories he outlined in April 1917. Now, however, a new chapter in the history of the Mass Terror was about to open: the campaign against the nationalities.

During the early years of the Soviet Union the lot of the national minorities, particularly those located within the Russian, Belorussian and Ukrainian Republics, was a happy one indeed. They formed an intricate mosaic of people with different ethnic origins, from Poles, Rumanians and Bulgarians in the west to Balts and Finns in the north and Koreans in the east. More or less closed Jewish communities still existed, and even a scattering of some 200,000 Greeks. All these, and many others, were encouraged to develop their different cultures and national traditions, and efforts were made to settle them in compact national areas. Eleven such National Areas were created in the Russian Republic alone, such as the Finnish National Area of Kuivosovsk to the east of Leningrad with 75,000 inhabitants and the Korean National Area in the far east with a population of 300,000. National Soviets operated in these areas at all levels, teaching was carried on in the national language and Russian was taught as a foreign language. Officials, including judges and policemen, were required to learn the national language if they came from outside the area.

This relatively idyllic phase in the treatment of national minorities ended when the great purges began and all manifestations of independence came under suspicion. Even so, the minorities were probably no worse off than the rest of the population until international tension increased in the mid-thirties. The first to suffer wholesale as a community on purely ethnical grounds were the Koreans. As the Japanese threat grew on the Far Eastern frontiers the entire Korean population numbering some 300,000 souls was removed in 1937 from its settlement areas to the Uzbek and Kazakh Republics in Central Asia under conditions closely resembling the deportation of the kulaks a few years earlier. This became the pattern for dealing with ethnic groups which might present a security risk or which Stalin wished to punish during World War II and immediately after it. From the outbreak of war ethnic groups disappeared without official notice or acknowledgement and the first the Soviet public heard about their fate was when they were rehabilitated after the Twentieth Party Congress.

Statistical material about the local details of ethnic minorities was not published between 1934 and 1956, and the course of the Terror against the nationalities must therefore be inferred from very incomplete data and from eye-witness reports. It was the Poles who suffered most heavily.

Katyn is a wretched village some twelve miles west of Smolensk, so lost in the surrounding forests that few people except those who live there know that it exists. In April 1943 German soldiers made a gruesome discovery there: they came upon a mass grave. The half-rotted papers found among the corpses indicated that these were Polish soldiers who had come to a violent end and had been buried on the spot.

A German Commission of Investigation was sent out. Further graves were discovered, until the number of bodies approached 11,000. It was one of the most terrible discoveries of its kind ever made before the world came to hear of the German concentration camps. German propaganda had a field day: eminent criminologists and lawyers were taken to Katyn to inspect the graves. The find created tremendous excitement and remained a theme in German newspapers and radio until the collapse of Hitler's Reich.

A study of the documents indicated that the victims were Polish officers and suggested April 1941 as the time of their death. The officers had definitely been murdered – in some cases the bodies were still bound with ropes. It seemed clear that they had been liquidated after being arrested by the Soviet authorities. The Polish Government-in-Exile, then located in London, asked that the circumstances should be investigated by the International Red Cross, whereupon the Soviet Government broke off relations with it.

Soviet propaganda asserted that it was the Germans who had killed the officers in order to blacken the reputation of the Red Army. Further witnesses and experts were produced to establish that the mass murders had taken place in September 1941, after the German invasion of Russia, rather than before it. Katyn was included in the indictment of the chief German war criminals at the Nuremberg trial but no evidence was produced and the matter was allowed to lapse.

Very little doubt now remains that the Soviet Union was responsible for Katyn. The massacre fits well into war-time Soviet practice towards the nationalities. The restoration of an independent Poland was one of the Allied war aims, and from the moment that the Red Army entered the country the Soviet authorities had done all they could to eliminate all Poles who might provide independent leadership at the end of the war.

Soviet population statistics throw some light on the treatment of the Polish minority before and after the outbreak of war. Over four million Poles in the territory occupied by the Red Army following the Soviet-German Pact were added to the 627,000 Soviet citizens of Polish origin listed in the census of 1939, making a total of some five million Poles in the Soviet Union. War casualties were particularly heavy among the Polish population and 1·5 million Poles were repatriated after the end of the war, largely for resettlement in the former German province of Silesia. If every allowance is made for these losses the figure of 1·38 million Soviet citizens of Polish origin shown in the census of 1939 is still unnaturally low, bearing in mind that a large part of the occupied territory was retained by the Soviet Union. Over a million Poles at the very least are missing, and probably more.

There is a sinister coincidence between this figure and the estimate of between 1·4 and 1·6 million Poles deported in 1939–41 by GULAG as slave labour to the Siberian and Far Eastern concentration camps. The only accurate statistic available as an indication of the vast scale of these deportations is the release of 114,000 Poles from Soviet Forced Labour Camps in August 1941 to form a volunteer army under General Anders. The Soviet Union was desperately short of troops at that time, yet the Anders Army was sent to fight in Africa and Italy over a complicated and time-consuming route through Iran, so as to ensure that these Poles should find no opportunity of taking a hand in the liberation of their own country.

The next on the list for deportation were the Baltic nationalities. The Red Army marched into Estonia, Latvia and Lithuania in June 1941. All three countries had lost their independence in everything but name some months earlier, when Stalin's closest henchman at that time, the former head of the Leningrad Party Organisation Zhdanov, set up his headquarters in Tallinn, the Estonian capital, and began to organise subservient Governments there, as well as in Latvia and Lithuania. A little later Molotov told the Lithuanian Prime Minister who was visiting Moscow: 'You will see that it will take less than four months for the population of all the Baltic States to vote for incorporation in the

Soviet Union. You should see things as they are, and understand that small countries must vanish in future.'

The presence of the Red Army and of the NKGB which followed closely in its footsteps was an even more convincing argument for annexation. Documents captured by the Germans, and from them by the Americans, give a clearer picture of NKGB activities in Lithuania than is available from the other Baltic States. It can be assumed, however, that the course of events was the same in all three countries. It certainly led to the same result – the deportation of hundreds of thousands of local inhabitants.

On 23rd April 1941 Gladkov, the Head of the NKGB in Kaunas, the capital of Lithuania, gave comprehensive orders to his subordinates, most of them native Russians, to prepare for deportations. Lists of all suspects were to be drawn up, a suspect being any person who might prove to be an opponent of the regime if a German invasion took place.

A month later, Gladkov's deputy urged haste: 'I warn all Heads and Deputy Heads of NKGB District staffs that all those guilty of irresponsibly allowing evidence concerning counter-revolution-aries and anti-Soviet elements to accumulate will from now on be brought most strictly to account.' Two days later seventeen NKGB Districts were accused of still failing to submit black lists. The preparations were completed by the end of May and in each District a 'Troika' of three NKGB officials held all the evidence required for deportation. On 31st May Moscow was able to issue the following order: 'Persons with anti-Soviet tendencies who have taken part in active counter-revolutionary agitation are to be made ready for deportation to distant parts of the USSR. Carry out immediately.'

Railroad trucks were supplied. Squads of four armed men were detailed to collect two families each. Their instructions were explicit: 'Weapons must be carried at the ready and rifles are to be loaded.' NKGB Headquarters feared a general rising if the plans for deportation became known, but the operation was carried out on 6th June without a hitch. Each deportee was allowed to take up to one hundred kilograms of personal belongings and families were told that men and women must pack their luggage separately, because a health inspection would be carried out before embark-ation. This was merely another measure to prevent disturbances; men and women were separated at the rail sidings before being deported to Krasnoyarsk, the mines at Karaganda and the area round Tomsk in Siberia. It is estimated that 61,000 Estonians, 34,000 Latvians and 38,000 Lithuanians were uprooted in this operation alone.

The list of nationalities subjected to similar treatment because the Soviet authorities regarded them as unreliable, or simply inconveniently located, is tragically long. Karelians and other Finnish minorities settled too close to the Finnish border, Rumanians, German settlers on the Volga, Kalmuks, Crimean Tartars, Caucasian peoples, such as the Chechen, the Ingush and the Karachai, and others of whose fate we know little or nothing. The only detailed evidence at our disposal is that which can be inferred from population statistics. The census of 1939, for instance, shows that 253,000 Karelians then lived in the Soviet Union and that by 1959 their numbers had shrunk to 167,000 of which 101,000 were women and 66,000 men. The disproportion between the sexes suggests that it was mainly able-bodied men who were deported as slave labour.

It might be thought that some at least of these reductions in numbers are due to assimilation into the Russian population, but Soviet statistics indicate both the ethnic origin and the language spoken by the members of each minority. For example, out of the 167,000 Karelians listed in the 1959 census, 45,000 are shown as Russian-speaking. The disappearance of hundreds of thousands of non-Russians from the Soviet census returns therefore points to their physical liquidation through death in exile as slave labourers. The numbers involved are so great and the injustice of punishing entire nationalities for the actual or, more often, potential disaffection of a few of their members is so monstrous that a Western mind finds it difficult to accept the facts about the Soviet treatment of non-Russian minorities from the mid-thirties to Stalin's death.

A collection of laws and decrees promulgated since 1938 was published in Moscow in 1956. It contains the following decree, dated 25th June 1946:

> During the Great Patriotic War, when the peoples of the USSR were heroically defending their honour and the independence of the Fatherland in battle against the Fascist German invader, many Chechen and Crimean Tartars, prompted by German agents, joined

volunteer units organised by the Germans, conducted operations against Red Army units together with the German forces and organised, also at German instigation, sabotage units for operations in the rear against the Soviet authorities, while the majority of the population of the Checheno-Ingush Autonomous Socialist Soviet Republic and the Autonomous Crimean Republic did nothing to resist these traitors to the Fatherland.

For this reason the Chechen and the Crimean Tartars were resettled in other parts of the USSR, where land was assigned to them and the requisite State assistance for land development was made available. On a motion of the Praesidium of the Supreme Soviet, the Checheno-Ingush ASSR was abolished and the Autonomous Crimean Republic was converted into the Crimean District by decrees of the Supreme Soviet. . . .

The treatment of the Chechen and the Crimean Tartars is the worst in the record of Soviet measures against ethnic minority groups because it was retrospective and vindictive. The vicious concept of family responsibility, so prevalent during the Great Purge, was extended to cover entire nationalities. Moreover, the uprooting and deportation of every individual belonging to an ethnic group which was as helpless in the face of the Soviet regime as it had been under German occupation has hardly any parallel in history since Asian tyrants transported subject people in Biblical times. Hundreds of thousands lost their ancestral homeland and tens of thousands perished on the way to slave labour settlements merely because they belonged to a nation and spoke a language that were considered 'hostile to the Soviet Union'.

Soviet citizens of German origin present a special case in the treatment of minorities, not only because they underwent massive repression – which is understandable in the circumstances – but because they were the first ethnic group to be rehabilitated after Stalin's death and the only one to have increased in numbers. The Soviet census of 1939 shows 1·4 million Germans, nearly sixty per cent of whom lived in rural settlements – the Autonomous Republic of Volga Germans alone had a population of over 600,000. Repression began in 1934–35, and was stimulated by the rise of Nazism with its doctrine of the 'Drang nach Osten' – The Thrust to the East. German schools were closed, German publications suspended and German ceased to be the official language of autonomous districts and local institutions. At the outbreak of war the Autonomous Republic of Volga Germans was abolished by a decree of the Praesidium of the Supreme Soviet and instructions were issued for 'the resettlement of Germans residing in the Volga area'.

This decree was never published and its existence was officially acknowledged only in 1964, when the Supreme Soviet reversed its verdict. The reason given for resettlement in 1942 had been that 'large groups of Soviet citizens of German origin had actively helped Hitlerite Germany', but the Supreme Soviet stated twenty-three years later that 'these accusations have proved to be un-founded and represent an arbitrary act of the Stalinist Cult of Per-sonality'. In reality, according to the Supreme Soviet, 'the majority of the German population, together with the entire Soviet people, contributed by its labour during the Great Patriotic War to victory over Fascist Germany and has taken an active part in the building of Communism in recent years'. Rehabilitation did not give the Volga Germans back their Autonomous Republic, but it may have done something to improve the lot of the German minority as a whole. According to census figures, and contrary to the statistical trend in all other Soviet minority groups, the German population in the Soviet Union increased by twenty-seven per cent between 1939 and 1959 in spite of the departure of some 200,000 Germans when Hitler's armies withdrew from the Soviet Union. The average rate of increase of the population for the Soviet Union as a whole was nine per cent during the same period and the unnatural growth of the German minority must therefore come from Germans who failed to leave the Baltic States, Eastern Poland and East Prussia before these were annexed. To them must be added an unknown number of Germans deported from Hungary, Rumania and the Eastern Zone, as well as prisoners of war who failed to return. These people are lost and exist, in so far as the outside world is concerned, only in Soviet statistics.

CHAPTER THIRTEEN

The School of Violence

EARLY in February 1940 a truckload of convicts left Moscow,
containing twenty-eight men and two women locked
behind bars. They could not tell where they were going
because there were no windows, but in other ways the truckload
had nothing in common with the usual prison convoys that
streamed out of Moscow. Their rations were princely – butter,
cheese, tinned foods, even cigarettes. The two women had even
been taken to a hairdresser before leaving. They found the complete change in their circumstances difficult to grasp and wondered
what new mean trick by the NKVD was in store for them. Only
a few weeks earlier these people had vegetated like caged animals
in Siberian penal camps – enemies of the State, saboteurs, counter-
revolutionaries with forced labour sentences of up to twenty years –
'A week ago still in a filthy mud hut in Siberia, firmly convinced
that one would never get out alive. . . .'[1]

Suddenly, without any obvious reason, they did get out, at
least as far as Butyrki Prison in Moscow which most of them had
left earlier on their way to the east. Margarete Buber-Neumann,
one of the two women, was put into a cell containing twenty-five
clean beds with spotless bed linen. When she had last seen that
cell one hundred and ten women had been packed into it, it was
crawling with bedbugs and the yells of a warder had woken the
inmates at three in the morning. Now she could have two eggs
for breakfast and there was as much hot water in the shower room
as she might want.

When the truckload assembled after about two weeks of
'readjustment' it included, apart from Margarete Buber-Neumann
and Betty Colberg as the only two women, a number of Jewish
refugees, German Communists and Austrian Schutzbund members who had fled to the Soviet Union after the abortive Civil
War in 1934.

Nobody in the group had the slightest idea of their destination
until after three days they reached the bridge at Brest-Litovsk on
the border between Soviet and German parts of occupied Poland.

A soldier marched slowly up and down the bridge. As he drew near I recognised the cap of the Nazi ss. The NKVD officer drew a list from a long, light-brown leather pouch. He was a whole head taller than the ss officer. His face was frozen and mask-like, as they say in pornographic novels. I couldn't catch the names he read out, but I heard him mention Buber-Neumann. . . .

The truck with twenty-eight men and two women was by no means the only one of its kind. Stalin was purging his prisons and camps of inmates who were probably more inconvenient to him than any others: Communist leaders, Spanish Civil War fighters, Comintern agents, non-Russian Party officials who, full of enthusiasm, had taken refuge in the land of their dreams only to encounter the realities of Soviet life. After years of NKVD treatment they might have thought that they knew everything about the Stalinist way of Communism, but the fact that Stalin's NKVD could hand them over to the Gestapo came as a final and terrible surprise.

Margarete Buber-Neumann, the child of a well-off Potsdam family, first married the son of the great Jewish theologian and sociologist Martin Buber, and then the German Communist leader Heinz Neumann, whom she accompanied to the Soviet Union in 1935. Neumann was arrested in Moscow in April 1937 at the Hotel Lux, the living quarters of the permanent Comintern staff.

In Moscow the atmosphere caught one by the throat. Former political friends no longer dared to visit each other. One needed a pass to get into the Hotel Lux and every visitor was registered in. The NKVD was everywhere. Telephones in the private rooms were monitored: we always noticed the crackling sound as soon as communication was established. Needless to say, all mail was opened. The fear of being watched became so great that when good friends did visit each other they would whisper:
'Have you searched your room carefully to make sure that they haven't put in a listening device somewhere? Isn't there perhaps a microphone somewhere? In the lamp, perhaps? Or in the telephone?' A man I knew once took all the electric points to pieces looking for microphones.
There was not a single émigré who had not 'deviated' at some time or other during the past ten years and so the 'Personnel Section of the Comintern' and the 'International Control Commission' had everybody in their clutches.

These people were ardent Communists who had proved themselves as clandestine organisers, as street-fighters and in jail – the
vanguard of the Comintern. It was their bad luck that Stalin
renounced the concept of World Revolution and decided on
'Socialism in One Country' instead. Most of them gradually came
to understand during the thirties that the Comintern was
increasingly an instrument of Soviet foreign policy at the expense
of the workers' interests elsewhere.

Moscow's watchword became: 'The Soviet Union is the home
of all workers. What is good for the Soviet Union must also be
good for proletarians everywhere.' Each twist of Soviet domestic
policy, every campaign against the 'rightists' or 'leftists', however
irrelevant it might be, was blindly reflected in Comintern policy
and enforced by an army of time-serving bureaucrats. The
foreign Communists did their best to follow the Party line, but
they could not always suppress their misgivings: and the twists and
turns of the Party line were so extreme that what was true and
correct one day was often wrong and treasonable the next.

For many foreign Communists the Spanish Civil War came as
the breaking point, at first because of Soviet hesitations about aid
to the Spanish Government, and later over the methods of the
Communist bid for power at any cost. The intrigues against the
Socialists, the Anarchists and the Trotskyists took priority over
the successful conduct of the war. And at the end, Stalin suddenly
dropped the cause of the Spanish Government and became Hitler's
ally.

This was too much even for some of the most faithful supporters, and the Comintern threatened to become a focus of disaffection and possibly a danger for Stalin's regime. In any case,
Yezhov and his henchmen were extending the Great Purge to
foreigners in the natural course of events. The domestic situation
was far from satisfactory twenty years after the October Revolution, and although the people were cowed, they grumbled. In
these circumstances, men like Heinz Neumann and El Campesino,
who knew the worst about Soviet activities abroad as the mass
of Soviet citizens did not know it, were dangerous. The potential
opposition in the Comintern had to be liquidated. Only the
yes-men were left, such as Gerö, Ulbricht, Togliatti and Thorez.

The test to which the ideological pliability of such men was
put stood Stalin in good stead a few years later when he was able

to send them back into post-war Europe with the certain knowledge that he could rely on them whatever happened. But at this
time the greatest trial for International Communism was yet to
come – the pact with Hitler.

Shortly after the outbreak of war in September 1939 Harry
Pollitt, the leader of the British Communist Party, published a
pamphlet which declared that: 'The British Communist Party
supports this war because it regards it as a just war.' The pamphlet
added that – 'it would be a betrayal of everything that our fore-
fathers have achieved during long years of struggle against
capitalism' if one were to stand aside while the Fascist Beast
rampaged through the whole of Europe. Less than two weeks
later the slogan changed and became: 'Put an End to The Capitalist
War.'

   This sudden and complete alteration of course by the Communist
Party can be seen most clearly in Britain because the political
traditions of the country allowed those concerned to speak their
minds more openly. The first reaction of British Communists was
a natural one – any war against Hitler and National Socialism must
be a just war. The shock of the Hitler-Stalin Pact had been
absorbed. The Western Democracies had done their best to drive
the Soviet Union into isolation for twenty years: they had com-
promised with Hitler and Mussolini. It was easy enough to argue
that the pact was no more than an act of despair by the Soviet
Union, undertaken in self-defence, because nothing was then
known of the Secret Protocol by which Hitler and Stalin had
divided Eastern Europe between them.

   Three weeks later, when the Soviet Union took its share of
German loot and occupied Eastern Poland, everything changed.
The Protocol was still a closely guarded secret but its effects were
there for all to see. Stalin may have hoped that the Fascist
States and the Western Democracies would inflict such damage
on each other that at the end of the war the Soviet Union would
emerge as the real victor without firing a shot, but this argument
was not likely to appeal to British public opinion, now at war. In
any case, the Communist Parties of Europe were given no time
to work out their own position in the matter because the new line
came from Moscow: the war was imperialist and therefore 'unjust'.
The Central Committee of the British Communist Party adopted

a resolution whereby not only the Nazi aggressors, but the reactionary English, French and Polish Governments were held jointly responsible for the conflict. Only two members of the Central Committee dissented.

Matters were different in France, if only because the French Communist Party was a real political force. This made it all the more difficult to reconcile the Party's rank and file to the Pact. Twenty-one out of seventy-two Communist Deputies in Parliament left the Party, as well as one of the two Communist Senators. Those who were left unanimously supported the war effort until the Red Army's entry into Poland, closely followed by the return from Moscow of Raymond Guyot, one of the Party's leaders. The war was now declared to be imperialistic. As a gesture of protest, Maurice Thorez deserted from his army unit and the French Communist Party celebrated the event by a pamphlet stating that the Imperialist War was a war against the people and that the people would refuse to fight it.

The changes in the Party line were difficult enough to keep up with in France or Britain, but Communists in Nazi dominated territories were set the most difficult problem of all. *Die Welt*, a German language paper published in Stockholm by the Comintern, carried the following slogan: 'Stalin's Pact is not with Hitler, it is with the German people against Hitler.' According to *Die Welt* the underground struggle against National Socialism must go on. The Soviet Union had concluded the Pact in sheer self-defence. Let Hitler lose the war – the more quickly he lost it, the better things would be for the Soviet Union, and the downtrodden proletariat everywhere.

This was a neat piece of argument, but it forced ordinary Communists to indulge in impossible mental contortions. They were to go on fighting, while Stalin outwardly betrayed everything that was sacred to Communists, and they were to prepare Hitler's fall while Stalin reaped the benefits of Hitler's imperialist adventures.

Seen in the light of later events, the Hitler-Stalin Pact and the changing Party line can be regarded as part of a deliberate plan whereby Soviet foreign policy and the activities of the Comintern would operate, separately at first and then together, to bring Eastern Europe under Soviet control. The pattern of events between 1939 and 1945 bears an uncanny resemblance to the ideas put forward by a little-known Russian historian, Nikolai Danilevsky, during the reign of Alexander II, sixty years earlier. In a series of articles published in the periodical *Zarya* in 1869–70 under the title 'Russia and Europe' Danilevsky formulated what he considered should be the aims of Russian foreign policy and his proposals became the guide lines of the regime until its fall. Russia was to replace the decaying Turkish and Austro-Hungarian Empires in Eastern Europe; create a federation of vassal Slav States incorporating the non-Slav populations in Hungary and Rumania; and secure access to the Mediterranean by conquering Constantinople.

Stalin may never have read Danilevsky's writings but his foreign policy closely followed them, just as it pursued the aims of Russian imperial policy in the Far East by establishing Soviet domination over Outer Mongolia and extending Soviet influence into China and Korea. Only the methods had changed – subversion and Terror were added to military power as the means of conquest. All three were brought into action after the Allied victory over Germany in 1945.

On 30th April 1945, the day of Hitler's death, a Soviet aircraft delivered a group of ten men at an airfield in East Germany. The leader of the group was Walter Ulbricht, a carpenter from Leipzig and former Communist deputy in the Reichstag. He later served in Spain as a Political Commissar charged with the supervision of German-speaking recruits in the training camp of the International Brigades. During the war his difficult task had been to explain the twists and turns of Stalin's policy to the Communist members of the German Underground movement in the pages of *Die Welt*. His present assignment was to prepare the Communist take-over in the Soviet-occupied zone of Germany.

The most interesting member of the group was also the youngest, Wolfgang Leonhard, twenty-three years old and born in Vienna, who went to the Soviet Union with his mother at the age of thirteen. She was arrested a year later and deported during the *Yezhovchina*. In 1949 he broke with Communism and wrote *Child of the Revolution*, which remains the best and clearest account of the Communist system for the layman.

As a nineteen-year-old, Leonhard was sent to the mining district of Karaganda in Kazakhstan, 2,400 kilometres from Moscow as the crow flies, in one of the innumerable convoys of

Germans proscribed from residing in towns after the outbreak of war. The circumstances of their deportation were easier than those of the convicts of every kind, including deviationists from the Comintern, who had preceded them in the area.

> Our cases had been loaded on camel-carts and ox-carts. The women and invalids were also put in the carts. The rest of us followed silently beside the carts. It was a melancholy picture – a long trail of exhausted human beings, straggling over the country-side after twenty-two days in overcrowded goods wagons, now sent to live in a place which ten years before had been a place of exile for kulaks. . . .[2]

Wolfgang Leonhard left Karaganda after a few months for the Comintern Training Centre at Ufa, 1,150 kilometres east of Moscow. Training had been a major concern of the Bolsheviks from the start. Rosa Luxemburg's warning about the price the Bolsheviks would have to pay for failing to educate the working class came true as soon as the professional revolutionaries seized power in 1917. The task of running and developing a huge country as well as keeping the bourgeois experts under control proved too much for the thin line of Party officials. Training was not just a matter of ensuring strict conformity to the Party line, it meant providing general education. In 1927–28, for instance, nearly three-quarters of a million members and candidate-members of the Party attended some 10,000 courses.

The Comintern Training Centre at Ufa was a high school of conspiratorial techniques and the exploitation of Terror. Its purpose was to form men and women who could be sent out as emissaries to conquer post-war Europe from the roots upwards. Among the subjects taught were methods of partisan warfare, the preparation of illegal literature and other clandestine techniques, including the all-important business of subverting the 'People's Councils'.

These People's Councils were designed to provide provisional authorities in conquered countries when the normal machinery of the State had collapsed. It was planned to set them up not only in Germany, where defeat would inevitably mean the end of every sort of constituted authority, but in all countries overrun by the Red Army, many of which had Governments in exile in London. The aim was to model the People's Councils on the Russian Soviets, and thereby confront the returning politicians with an accomplished fact. The Comintern was well aware that only a tiny majority of the population in these countries favoured Communism; democratic forms must therefore be observed to start with, so that a gradual take-over of power could follow later.

At the Comintern Training Centre such plans were still at a fairly rudimentary stage and dealt with the establishment of 'clandestine' Councils to stimulate resistance to Hitler on a wide political front. It was regarded as most important that the initiative for the creation of the Councils should be seen to come from the Communists – The Vanguard of Anti-Fascism. Support for various political parties and shades of opinion among the population as a whole could not be accurately measured under wartime conditions, and it was therefore likely to be easy for Communist activists to organise illegal committees. If representatives of other parties and political groupings could be induced to join them, the People's Councils would emerge at the liberation as representing the nation. The first free elections would, of course, reveal the true state of public opinion but, given proper handling, their date could be deferred until the electoral procedure was under Communist control.

Leonhard describes how the pupils at the Comintern Centre were taught to organise Councils and to draft ministers of religion, lawyers, Party members and other representatives of the public into them, working from directories and local statistical information. The more intelligent pupils may not have taken such training exercises too seriously, but these techniques were shown to work in practice when several People's Councils turned into national governments in the wake of the Red Army's advance across Europe. In Austria, for instance, Communists held only two posts in the Provisional Government formed in April 1947 but they controlled the key areas of Education and Internal Affairs. Responsibility for education put not only the schools but all printing facilities into their hands and enabled them to launch the *Wiener Tageszeitung*, the first post-war newspaper to appear in Austria. The Ministry of the Interior placed the police and gendarmerie at their disposal, together with the complete records of the Security Service. A few months later the first general elections demonstrated that the Communist Party had no real hold over the population: they won only four seats out of 165, although more than a third of the country was under Soviet occupation.

The most important – and most unpleasant – feature of the course at Ufa was the method used to drill the trainees into absolute spiritual subjection. Leonhard, who was known under the cover name of Linden, describes an 'improvised' trial at which one of his fellow pupils began to read out a long list of remarks made by Leonhard during the previous weeks, such as:

'When we came back from wood-cutting on the evening of 6th October at about 7.30 some comrades from the Spanish group passed us. Linden then said to Forster that some of the Spanish girls were very pretty.'

The remark might seem harmless enough, but the chairman of the meeting made very heavy weather of it:

> One has only to look at the facts. In the middle of the war, when we are engaged in a life and death struggle against the Fascist criminals, when the entire Soviet people is sacrificing everything to achieve victory and national independence, the Party gives Comrade Linden the opportunity to study and prepare himself for the struggle ahead under ideal conditions. The Party has the right to expect that Linden's every effort will be directed to that purpose, that all his strength will be devoted to that aim, that every minute will be used for his studies and that all his thoughts will be concentrated on the coming battle. And what, in fact, is Linden thinking of? He is thinking of pretty Spanish girls and so puts the interests of his ego above those of the Party. . . .

The chairman spoke so earnestly and so accusingly that, as Leonhard recalls: 'It all seemed so logical that by this time I felt myself guilty of having committed these crimes.'

The case of the Spanish girls was merely one out of many quoted by Leonhard's fellow pupil and each of them was solemnly discussed until it had grown into a major crime. The session went on and on. The accused was asked to criticise himself. His self-criticism was considered inadequate, because he still failed to recognise the full seriousness of his faults, and so the entire process was repeated in front of all the students in his year, who were invited to comment on his behaviour one by one.

The purpose of this and other conditioning techniques was threefold. Fear was to be instilled in every individual: there were watchers everywhere; every incautious word would reach higher authority. It was futile to lie. Only silence was safe. Each man must fear his neighbour and the slightest attempt to deviate or to voice a subversive thought would be crushed without delay.

Secondly, every individual's self-confidence must be broken. He must feel guilty about his failure to do enough for the Party. When this sense of guilt had become deep enough it would drive him to make up for his shortcomings by more intense loyalty and to strive for results above the average.

Finally, these techniques made fear and guilt a communal reaction among the group as a whole. When one Comrade confessed his faults the rest would become aware of their own guilty thoughts. They might not be fully convinced or see the whole enormity of their own errors, but they would learn not to put them into words, to be afraid.

Leonhard quotes the example of another pupil, Willy, a former worker from Berlin who had fought in the Spanish Civil War. The class was rehearsing rules of behaviour for clandestine Communists in the German armed forces. They were told the fundamental principle of 'conspiratorial' work: security must be preserved at all costs, even if this means sharing in crime. Then a problem was put to Willy: 'A small Army unit to which a member of the illegal organisation belongs is ordered to set houses on fire and shoot Russian women and children. What should he do? Does the basic principle of underground work still remain in force when it is a matter of atrocities against the Soviet population?' Willy was confused: 'Well, I don't know . . . It seems to me that even in such a difficult position . . . probably . . . perhaps, even in a case like that, one must not give away the illegal organisation.' The instructor's verdict was sharp: 'That is not a political mistake – it is treason. Treason against the anti-Fascist struggle, treason against the German Workers' Movement, treason against the Party, treason against the first country of Socialism, against the Soviet Union.' Leonhard later heard that Willy finished up in a concentration camp.

Willy had been deliberately trapped in order to show with absolute clarity that neither the principles of underground work nor any other considerations mattered when the welfare of the Soviet Union was at stake.

The people trained in this way would sooner or later return home as Soviet agents and would one day give orders running counter to their own country's interests. Their training ensured that they would not hesitate, because the Soviet system had become their only home. This is why so many Communists in post-war Eastern Europe unflinchingly carried out even the most absurd and unnatural orders from Moscow. It is why Slansky and Clementis were executed in Czechoslovakia and Rajk in Hungary. It is also the reason why Tito and the Yugoslav Communists broke away.

This training technique was invented when Lenin solved the problem of how a minority could seize power and keep it, and when the Russian Communists accepted the principle that Terror could legitimately be used to suppress every manifestation of mental and physical resistance. Ever since the October Revolution an ever-growing army of officials was busy perfecting the use of the Terror as an instrument of government. There were Party bureaucrats dealing with awkward questions, Comintern agents breaking the resistance of nationally-minded foreign Communists, NKVD officials who must produce confessions. At first Terror was used in self-defence, then it became a weapon of attack.

But Terror has its own logic; once it is brought into play those who use it only too easily fall victim to it. By its very nature it generates resistance from below and puts its authors into danger. They must take seriously even the slightest sign of independence. They are threatened from every side and must constantly invent better ways of holding down the world at large. When the Soviet Union exported these methods, it eventually discovered that the world at large could not be held down for ever.

SOURCES

1. Margarete Buber-Neumann, *Als gefangene bei Stalin und Hitler* (Stuttgart, 1948).

2. Wolfgang Leonhard, *Child of the Revolution* (Henry Regnery Company, New York, 1959).

CHAPTER FOURTEEN

The Revolt Against Violence

THE old city of medieval and baroque at the heart of the very modern Polish capital has been rebuilt with loving care. In it stands the Museum of the Polish Resistance, a highlight of any guided tour of Warsaw. After paying tribute to the undoubted heroism of the Polish Underground Army a visitor from the West finds it difficult to avoid asking why the Red Army which stood for nearly four weeks on the right bank of the Vistula, in the suburb of Praha, should have made no serious effort to cross to the left bank and come to the aid of the Polish patriots fighting a desperate battle among the ruins and in the sewers of the city. The official answer is wordy and unconvincing. Is the real answer that the Soviet Union allowed the Polish Underground Army to bleed to death in order to eliminate the last remnants of those who might have claimed to represent an independent Poland?

The Red Army's summer offensive opened in Southern Poland and Galicia on 13th July 1944. Brest-Litovsk fell on 28th July. Lwow had fallen earlier. Grodno and Bialystok were taken on 16th and 18th July. The beginning of the massed attack on Warsaw was clearly only a matter of days.

On 1st August the Polish Underground Army rose in the city, so that the Poles themselves should liberate their own capital and also to avoid the destruction of Warsaw in the course of street fighting between the Russians and the Germans. The leader of the rising, General Komorowski, better known under his cover name of Bor, reckoned to hold out only a few days until the Red Army moved in. He also hoped that the Russians would meet with slight resistance because the Germans had their hands full dealing with the rising.

General Bor was proved wrong. Stanislaw Mikolajczyk, the leader of the Polish Peasant Party and Prime Minister of the London Government-in-Exile, reached Moscow at the end of July. He intended to re-open diplomatic relations with the Soviet Union, broken off a year earlier when General Sikorski, Mikolajczyk's predecessor, demanded an International Red Cross investigation of the dreadful discoveries at Katyn. In the meantime Moscow had promoted the foundation of a Union of Polish Patriots and recruited an Army of Liberation from prisoners of war and deportees. The Western Allies welcomed these steps as contributions to the war effort, but the Polish exiles in London knew that Russia was not given to acting unselfishly in Poland, and they feared for the future.

Four years earlier, just before the conclusion of the Hitler-Stalin Pact, Marshal Voroshilov had told the members of a Franco-British military mission in Moscow that the Soviet Union would only act against Hitler in concert with the West if the Red Army were allowed to march through Poland. The French and British agreed, but the Polish leader, Rydz-Smigly, refused and said: 'With the Germans we risk our freedom. With the Russians we will lose our souls.'

On the eve of the German invasion Rydz-Smigly's remark sounded criminally silly. 1944 showed that he had been right. Mikolajczyk, faced with the demand to recognise the Soviet organised shadow Government of Poland known as the Lublin Committee and reach a compromise with it, refused to yield. Churchill told the House of Commons that the obstinacy of the London Government-in-Exile had sunk the hopes of a reconciliation between it, the Lublin Committee and the Soviet Government even further.

The Lublin Committee developed from the People's National Council founded in Warsaw in 1943 by Boleslaw Bierut, a veteran Communist and an official of the Comintern. The Council derived its support mainly from the Polish Workers' (i.e. Communist) Party, while the Union of Polish Patriots was recognised by the Soviet Government as the only genuine representative of the will of the Polish people. When the Red Army crossed the former Polish frontier in July 1944 the People's National Council declared itself a Provisional Government with the support of the Union of Patriots, but it was not given full recognition by the Western Allies. Its Chairman was a Socialist, Osobka-Morawski, and only four out of its fourteen other members were Communists. Communists, however, were responsible for Public Security and Education. The lessons taught at the Comintern Training Centre were being applied.

The Warsaw Rising had just started when Mikolajczyk reached Moscow, but the Soviet Government was less interested in helping the Polish Underground than in issuing an ultimatum. It demanded that the London Government should merge with the Lublin Committee, four seats out of eighteen being reserved for Mikolajczyk's group in the future Coalition Government.

Negotiations continued and so did the Warsaw Rising. When the Red Army at last reached the Praha suburb in September it stopped for no obvious military reason, and made no attempt to cross into the city or to encircle it. On 2nd October resistance ceased inside Warsaw after an epic struggle lasting sixty-two days. The Soviet Government was thereby rid of the Polish Underground Army. From then on the Polish people must look to the Red Army for their liberation.

While the sterile negotiations between the Allies about the rights of the London Government and the holding of free elections dragged wearily on month after month, the Ministry of Public Security set about preparing a simpler solution. Leading members of the opposition began to disappear, because as Molotov explained to Allied representatives, they had infringed Soviet laws for the protection of the Red Army. A number of senior members of the Polish Underground were tried under these laws and sentenced by a military court in Moscow in June 1945. When the American Ambassador in Warsaw protested against the suppression of Press freedom, Bierut replied that he had no intention of allowing the Fascist enemies of the Government to destroy it. Although Mikolajczyk and five other members of the Peasant Party were given ministerial posts, the elections kept on being deferred; the Austrian elections in November 1945 had shown that even military occupation and Communist control of Public Security did not guarantee a Communist success at the polls. The American Ambassador reported in March 1946 that the Bierut Government could only maintain itself in power with the support of the Red Army and the NKVD-dominated Security Police, and by the use of Terror.

The Polish Government's basic problem was simple enough; so long as an independent, non-Communist Peasant Party existed, the Communists could not risk free elections or impose the economic programme demanded by Moscow. Terror was the only way of resolving this difficulty and the 30,000 prisoners given amnesty in 1956 as a result of destalinisation provide some indication of its scale.

The Socialists were eventually persuaded to put up a common list of candidates with the Communists after Sciborek, a leader of the anti-Communist faction of the Socialist Party, had been murdered by a conveniently unidentified assassin. The Government also staged the trial of Colonel Rzepecki, the best known among the surviving leaders of the Underground Army. When the elections at last took place in January 1947 the Socialist-Communist Alliance, reinforced by two smaller parties, obtained more than nine million votes. Mikolajczyk, who had steadfastly refused to accept a fixed proportion of Parliamentary seats on the common list, secured only a little more than a million votes.

In October 1947 Mikolajczyk fled the country. So did Kopiel, the leader of the Christian Workers Party. Several other opposition leaders were arrested before they could escape. The first act of the Polish tragedy had ended with the Warsaw Rising. The curtain now fell on the second act; meanwhile, the Soviet Union extended the methods it had tried out in Poland to the remainder of Eastern Europe.

On 23rd February 1948 the Communist Minister of Defence, General Svoboda, assured the President of Czechoslovakia, Dr. Beneš, that no changes were impending among senior Army personnel. On the very next day twenty-five Generals were compulsorily retired and one of them, General Pika, a convinced anti-Communist, was arrested. Beneš was well aware that the dismissal of the Generals had been instigated by the Communist Prime Minister, Klement Gottwald, at Moscow's request. He said to Jan Masaryk, the Foreign Minister: 'One of these days all nations will rise and smash them!' He said to another Minister: 'I know the people in Moscow, their entire policy is a provocation to war. They will pay for this dearly. They are as blind as Hitler!'

Congresses of the Workers' Councils and of the Peasant Commissions had been called in mid-February. The slogan was: 'The Workers Demand the Nationalisation of Further Undertakings and a New Agrarian Reform.' The non-Communist members of the Government knew only too well what congresses of this kind foreshadowed, particularly as the Communist Minister of the Interior showed no inclination to restrain 'The March of the

People.' He mustered the Workers Militia to act as auxiliary police. The non-Communist Ministers resigned on 17th February. On the 21st Gottwald addressed a mass meeting of Communists in Prague. Workers' Councils sprang up everywhere on the Soviet model. Armed workers marched through the capital.

Beneš gave way when he found that with the dismissal of the Generals all hope that the Army would prevent a Communist take-over was gone. He accepted the formation of a Communist Government in which Masaryk, the son of the founder of the Czechoslovak Republic, still held his old post. On 10th March his body was found underneath the window of his study and argument has raged ever since (and with renewed vigour since the succession of Novotny by Dubcek in 1968) about whether his death was the result of murder or suicide. These events in Czechoslovakia were merely part of the great upheaval which began in East and South-East Europe during the early spring of 1947.

Hungary was first off the mark. Despite Soviet occupation and massive Communist propaganda, elections held in November 1945 gave an overwhelming victory to the Smallholders Party with nearly sixty per cent of the vote and 245 seats in Parliament. The Communists were not defeated as disastrously as in Austria a few weeks later, but they only secured 70 seats. At the end of May 1947 the Prime Minister, Ferenc Nagy, went to Switzerland on leave and sent his resignation from there. In the next Government half of the Ministers were Communists. President Zoltan Tildy retired a year later, after his son-in-law had been indicted for treason. The next to be arrested for high treason and currency offences was the Primate of Hungary, Cardinal Mindszenty.

In Bulgaria, Nikola Petkoff, the leader of the Peasant Party which had obtained thirty per cent of the votes at the elections in October 1946, was arrested in June 1947 and sentenced to death two months later. The Peasant Party was dissolved after his execution. A year later the Bulgarian Social Democrats merged with the Communists and Lulceff, their leader who opposed the merger, was imprisoned.

From Rumania the Peasant Party leader Iuliu Maniu directed a burning appeal to world opinion against the Communist Terror in his country and was arrested a few days later. King Michael was forced to abdicate in December 1947 and went into exile. In

February 1948 all remaining left-wing political groups in Rumania were incorporated in the Communist Party.

Poland was last on the list of complete Communist take-overs. The Polish Socialists were finally absorbed into the Communist Party in December 1948.

In the Soviet-occupied zone of Germany the mergers had taken place even earlier, in 1946. The members of the Socialist Party in West Berlin voted on the proposal for a merger and rejected it by a majority of eighty-two per cent. There was no vote in the Eastern Zone – the Chairman of the two Parties decreed the merger and created the German Unity Party (SED). Relatively free elections in September and October 1946 showed weak support for the SED. Its share of the votes even in traditionally left-wing areas such as Thuringia and Sachsen-Anhalt remained below fifty per cent. Out of 520 seats in all the Land Parliaments in the East Zone the SED held only 249.

The mosaic of countries involved in this upheaval – Hungary, Bulgaria, Rumania, Czechoslovakia, Poland, the East Zone of Germany – may be confusing at first sight, but there is a sameness about the course of events. The withdrawal of the German armies, followed by the collapse of local administrations, left anarchy in its wake. With the exception of Czechoslovakia the countries of Eastern Europe had not experienced a democratic regime of the Western kind for many years past, if ever, and nobody could forecast what political complexion the first provisional governments should have in order to represent the real opinions of the population.

It was amply clear to the Soviet authorities, however, that they could not count on Communist victories in genuinely free elections. Most of the countries concerned were predominantly agricultural and the supporters of the various Peasant Parties disliked any suggestion of collectivisation quite as much as they disliked the large estates of the old régime. Even in Czechoslovakia, a developed industrial country by Western standards, the Communists obtained only thirty-eight per cent of the poll at the elections of May 1946. Nor could the Communists indulge in open insurrections modelled on the Russian October Revolution, because the Soviet Government was allied to the Western Powers, needed their help and was therefore obliged to play the game according to democratic rules.

The Communists could therefore seize power only through subversion, first by obtaining the three key posts of Security, Education and Economic Affairs and then by arranging a merger with the Socialists and other left-wing parties which would enable them to ride into Parliament at the next election on the backs of their more popular confederates. By the first half of 1947 these tactics had met with only moderate success: everywhere except in East Germany the non-Communist workers' parties had retained a large measure of independence and other parties continued to operate in spite of growing difficulties.

These tactics changed abruptly towards the middle of 1947. Terror was intensified, opposition parties were dissolved and even the outward show of democratic legality was abandoned. Moscow felt that its newly established and still imperfectly consolidated empire was threatened from outside: this threat was embodied in a speech made on 5th June 1947 at Harvard University by General George C. Marshall, then U.S. Secretary of State in the Truman Administration.

Marshall, a former Army Chief of Staff, had become convinced, in the course of endless sterile Four-Power negotiations, that there was no hope of reaching an understanding between East and West. If the Soviet Union were allowed to establish itself unchallenged between the Baltic and the Adriatic, it would sooner or later extend its domination over all the war-ravaged countries of Europe. In what became known as the Marshall Plan he proposed that European countries should be helped to establish their independence on a sound economic foundation through industrial reconstruction financed by America. Dollar imperialism, as it was later called, was to prevent the conquest of the continent of Europe by the Soviet Union.

On 7th July 1947 Gottwald's Communist Government in Czechoslovakia decided to accept an invitation to attend the first Marshall Plan Conference in Paris. Two days later, Stalin told Gottwald and an official Czechoslovak delegation sharply and clearly that participation in the Marshall Plan would mean the end of friendship with the Soviet Union. Similar messages went to the Governments of all the other East European countries occupied by the Red Army.

In June 1946 Yatrov, a Soviet economic expert, was deep in

negotiations with a Yugoslav Government Commission in Belgrade. He felt throughly puzzled. A Communist Government had been in power in Yugoslavia from the moment of liberation. The Communist partisans fought the German Army to a standstill and founded their first National Committee at a time when Stalin still preferred to operate through non-Communist Liberation Councils so as to avoid trouble with his Western Allies. His disapproval was not lost on the Yugoslav leader, Josip Broz-Tito, formerly a secretary of the Comintern's Balkan Section and organiser of the Spanish Aid office in Paris during the Civil War. Tito had harboured heretical thoughts as far back as 1935.

> I knew that many things were wrong while I was working there; I witnessed a lot of careerism and elbow-pushing; I talked with collective farm members and noticed them nudging each other when they wanted to say something. People in Moscow somehow avoided each other, hesitated to speak. I was not in Moscow when the big purges occurred. But even in 1935 there were no end of arrests, and those who made the arrests were later themselves arrested. Men vanished overnight, and no one dared ask where they had been taken.
> My whole being rebelled against what I saw in Moscow.[1]

Despite these sombre memories Tito's own devotion to Communism was not in doubt, and he was stern enough in enforcing it. The special tribunals were busy in Yugoslavia at the time of Yatrov's visit in June 1946. After a show trial Draga Mihailovic, a rival but non-Communist partisan leader, was sentenced to death with twelve of his associates. Three months later it was the turn of Cardinal Stepinac, Primate of the Catholic Church and Archbishop of Zagreb, to receive a life sentence. What puzzled the Soviet expert was the stiff resistance which he encountered from the Yugoslav side in negotiating economic collaboration with the Soviet Union. The Yugoslav representatives were not willing to accept Moscow's proposals out of hand:

> After Tito's return from Moscow, negotiations were opened in August of that year for the foundation of joint-stock companies. From the outset it was plain what the Soviet Union wanted from us. The Russian representative Yatrov made it clearly understood that he had orders from his Government to found Soviet-Yugoslav joint-stock companies in Yugoslavia of a type which would on the one hand give the Soviet Union a monopoly in whole branches of our industry, and even in our economy in general, and on the

other would exploit Yugolsavia's natural resources and in particular her raw materials. This meant that we should have remained a source of raw materials for developed countries, with no opportunity to develop our own industry. And without the development of industry in our country, there would be no foundation for the building of socialism in Yugoslavia.

During negotiations Yatrov openly said, 'What do you need heavy industry for? In the Urals we have everything you need.'

'However, we stood firmly by the view that Yugoslavia's natural resources must be exploited . . .

According to Soviet plans, the value of the oilfields in Yugoslavia was not to be recognized as Yugoslavia's share in the undertaking; he invoked Marx, saying they were natural wealth with no direct social value.'

Yugoslavia provides only one example among many of the Soviet drive to take over the economies of Eastern European countries. The creation of Joint or Mixed Stock Companies is a feature of Soviet policies in all the territories occupied by the Red Army. By 1947 thirty per cent of the industrial production of the Eastern Zone of Germany, for instance, came from these Soviet Stock Companies, or SAGs. The Soviet contribution to the SAGs consisted of factories and the industrial equipment. In other words, the Soviet Union merely forbore to dismantle German industrial plant and ship it to Russia as reparations, although the levying of war damages is as contrary to Marx's teaching as the attribution of value to mineral resources.

These Soviet economic activities throw a different light on the wave of Terror and diplomatic intimidation which set in during 1947. So long as the Communist Party was not in absolute control Soviet economic penetration met with constant resistance. If the occupied countries had succeeded in rebuilding and developing their industries by means of Marshall Aid, the Soviet Union would have had to abandon all hope of incorporating them into its economy as sources of raw material and suppliers of industrial goods. There could be no economic domination without political control and economic domination was essential to the Soviet presence in Eastern Europe. The Communist Parties which during the twenties and thirties had been the shock-troops of Soviet foreign policy now became the executive organs of Soviet economic imperialism.

Statistics of East European trade tell a clear story. Sixty-nine per cent of Poland's foreign trade was with the West in 1947;

by 1951 sixty per cent of it was with the Soviet Union. Czechoslovak trade with Eastern Europe came to thirty-two per cent of total foreign trade in 1948, sixty-one per cent in 1951 and seventy-five per cent in 1954. The trend was similar all over Eastern Europe.

Innumerable examples illustrate how often the re-orientation of the Eastern European economies was to the disadvantage of the countries involved. Czechoslovakia, for instance, invested heavily in a direct railroad driven through the Tatra Mountains to the Soviet border which was of little benefit to her. The great tractor works at Kolben-Denik had by 1954 turned out over 50,000 tractors, of which fewer than 15,000 were made available to Czechoslovak agriculture.

Another drawback of slavishly copying the Soviet model was the indiscriminate application of ideology in the most inappropriate circumstances, such as the drive to eradicate the middle class, the artisans and the independent peasants. Czechoslovakia is essentially a country of small-scale private enterprise, but only 30,000 workers were left outside State-run enterprises by 1955. As a result, the food shortages in the towns, the lack of catering establishments and tailors' shops has been a constant source of complaint in the Czechoslovak Press.

In 1945 the Socialist Head of the Provisional Polish Government, Osobka-Morawski, declared that it would probably take fifty to a hundred years before a Socialist economy could be established. Three years later the first Polish Six Year Plan already existed as a draft designed to meet Soviet requirements. The next phase in the establishment of Soviet domination over Eastern Europe was well under way.

In June 1948 the conflict between Stalin and Tito came out into the open. Titoism was now both a dirty word and a dangerous trend among Communist leaders. It found very cautious expression in Poland in a report to the Polish Politburo by Wladislaw Gomulka, Secretary-General of the Party and Deputy Prime Minister. He dealt with the differences in the historical development of Polish and Russian Communism. The very mention of any such differences was controversial enough from Moscow's point of view, but the implications of the report went far beyond points of ideology. Nothing less was involved than the claim that Polish Communists had the right to achieve Socialism in their own country in their own way, in accordance with the economic and social facts of the Polish situation. In other words, Soviet demands which contradicted Polish interests should be resisted.

Gomulka was relieved of his post as Secretary-General of the Party in September 1948 and, soon afterwards, of his Government appointment. Moscow was giving notice that Tito must not be imitated. A year later, Gomulka and General Spychalski, who had been regarded as the representative of the Communist organisation in the Army, were excluded from the Party. This was followed by an announcement designed to surprise even the most hardened of Western observers: Marshal Rokossovsky, one of the most distinguished Soviet commanders in World War II, claimed his Polish origin and was transferred to the Polish Army as its Commander-in-Chief. He brought with him nearly 5,000 Soviet officers, mostly of Polish origin, who took up key appointments in the Polish General Staff and all the more important commands.

At the time of Gomulka's dismissal the Cold War was at its height. The German currency reform was closely followed by the blockade of Berlin. All Soviet communications with the East Zone and Berlin lay through Poland. It was the most vulnerable area for Soviet military and political strategy. When Rokossovsky was appointed the Federal German Republic had just been inaugurated; and the effects of this decision were highly unpredictable; both in international terms and in so far as the East Zone of Germany was concerned.

At the beginning of 1948 the resistance of National Communists to Soviet domination just missed being named after Georgi Dimitrov rather than after Tito. Dimitrov, a Bulgarian printing worker by origin, was one of the best known among Comintern leaders. After many years of subversive and terrorist activity, including a leading part in the armed rising of 1923 in Bulgaria, he became famous as one of the accused in the Reichstag Fire Trial in Berlin in 1933, where he defended himself so ably and courageously against charges trumped-up by the Nazis that he secured an acquittal. Shortly afterwards he was released by the Gestapo at the Soviet Government's request and became Head of the Comintern's Balkan Secretariat in Moscow.

When he returned to Bulgaria at the end of the war he was to all appearances a typical and absolutely reliable member of the Communist Old Guard, drilled to identify the interests of all Communists and all Communist-dominated countries with those of the Soviet Union.

At the beginning of 1948 Dimitrov went on a State Visit to Rumania. Tito had recently concluded treaties of friendship with Bulgaria, Rumania and Hungary and his personal friendship with Dimitrov, who had been his chief in the Balkan Secretariat, was a matter of common knowledge. All this led to a Press interview in Bucharest in the course of which the possibility of a future Balkan Federation was mentioned. Dimitrov replied:

> The question of a federation or confederation is premature for us. It is not on the agenda at present, and therefore this question has not been a subject of discussion at our conferences. When the question matures, and it must inevitably mature, then our peoples, the nations of people's democracy, Rumania, Bulgaria, Yugoslavia, Albania, Czechoslovakia, Poland, Hungary, and Greece, mind you, and Greece!—will settle it.

There was no mention of the Soviet Union. On the contrary, Dimitrov had stressed that 'our peoples will solve it'. On 29th January *Pravda* reacted with an indignant article which referred to 'a questionable and artificially created Federation' which these countries needed as little as they did a Customs Union. Two weeks later Molotov, acting as Stalin's spokesman, informed representatives of the Bulgarian and Yugoslav Party leaderships who had been summoned to Moscow that the Soviet Union refused to consider any plans for a union.

After a long and heated debate Dimitrov admitted, in the tones of a Young Communist practising self-criticism: 'It is true, we have committed an error. But we learn from such errors in matters of foreign policy.' Stalin replied: 'You are an old politician and have engaged in politics for over forty years. Now you just wish to correct errors. This is not a matter of errors; these are concepts which deviate from ours.' Finally, Stalin declared that there should be three Federations, not one – Poland and Czechoslovakia, Rumania and Hungary, Bulgaria and Yugoslavia.

Nothing came of these or of any other Federations. From the Soviet point of view any suggestion that the Satellite States should enter into any form of combination for their own benefit was a direct threat, because it implied the right to assert a separate existence. Only Yugoslavia succeeded in this, because she was not occupied by the Red Army and because Tito had a firm grip on the Party and the country. Her example was tempting for even the most loyal Eastern European Communists, all the more so because the economic situation was deteriorating throughout the area. These economic and political difficulties, on the other hand, drove the Soviet regime to tighten its hold over the Satellites even further at the end of the forties.

Terror as it had been perfected over many years in the Soviet Union now came into full force against all actual and potential dissenters. In September 1949 the former Hungarian Foreign Minister Laszlo Rajk was tried with six others and executed. In December Traicho Kostov, one of the Bulgarian Party leaders, and ten others were brought before a Special Tribunal in Sofia. Kostov suspected Yugoslavia of intentions to dominate Bulgaria, but he was accused of collaborating with Tito nevertheless. He too was executed, although he was one of the few to retract his confession in court. In November 1952, the former Secretary-General of the Czechoslovak Party, Rudolf Slansky, and thirteen others went the same way after a Show Trial.

As in the Soviet Union, the Show Trials were followed by the elimination of innumerable lesser officials while the Terror spread to the entire population of the Eastern European countries. People's Courts in Czechoslovakia were empowered to deal with 'individuals who endangered the establishment of the Popular Democratic Order or the economic life of the country'. Their jurisdiction was later extended to cover anything that might be construed as disaffection.

In Bulgaria the Minister of the Interior was empowered to proceed without trial against 'all enemies of the people', defined as covering everything from the politically unreliable to gamblers and prostitutes.

Rumania went so far as to decree that 'actions regarded as commonly dangerous may attract punishment even if they are not explicitly forbidden by law'.

All over Eastern Europe a citizen who had made himself officially undesirable was at the mercy of the authorities with or without trial. Slander, private vengeance, corruption and black-mail flourished. Fear became the only rule and stifled all initiative and fresh thinking, as well as every attempt at protest.

Purges of the Eastern European Communist Parties reduced their membership from over eight million in 1948 to barely six million in 1953. All that was now left at the top was a set of blindly faithful yes-men: Bierut in Poland, Rakosi in Hungary, Gottwald in Czechoslovakia and Ulbricht in East Germany.

Looking back today on political life in Eastern Europe since World War II one should remember that Titoism meant trial and execution in the late forties and that a Foreign Minister in office such as Rajk could not even confer with Western diplomats without risking at some later date an accusation that he was a CIA agent. Now, fifteen years after Stalin's death, the empire he forged by force of arms, ruthless Terror and massive economic pressure is crumbling. In January 1967 the Soviet Government protested sharply against 'militaristic and neo-Nazi forces' in the German Federal Republic and called upon 'the Governments, Parliaments and peoples of the world' to do everything in their power to ensure that these forces should not imperil peace. This protest failed to restrain the Rumanian Foreign Minister from visiting Bonn and establishing diplomatic relations with Western Germany. The Soviet protest did not even restrain *Scinteia*, the official newspaper of the Rumanian Communist Party, from commenting as follows on East German criticism of the new course in Rumanian foreign policy: 'Does the author of the article not know that the foreign policy of a Socialist country is decided by the Party and Government of that country and that Party and Government are accountable only to their own people?'

Twenty years earlier far less than this would have earned a death sentence. In the year of its fiftieth anniversary the children of the Bolshevik Revolution were taking their freedom. And the destruction of the rule of violence that Lenin invented and Stalin imposed goes on relentlessly. The Soviet rulers know it, or how else can one explain their savage reaction to the Czechoslovak reforms begun early in 1968? From the very start of the movement that displaced Novotny, the old Stalinist nominee, as ruler of Czechoslovakia, the new leaders of the Party pledged their loyalty to Communism, the Soviet Union and the military and economic organisation which Russia had built in Eastern Europe. And if they criticised this organisation in detail, Rumania had got away unscathed for several years with a great deal more. But the Czechoslovak Communists rejected the tyranny of violence, opened the prisons, abolished censorship and curbed the power of the secret police. To strike at these was to strike at the very heart of the system that Lenin had conceived, and the Soviet rulers knew it. To let these reforms go unpunished meant signing their own political death warrant. But the course of history is irreversible and tomorrow the Bolsheviks also will be on the move.

SOURCE
1. Vladimir Dedijer, *Tito Speaks* (Weidenfeld and Nicolson, London, 1953).

Part Five

THE WRECKER'S YARD

CHAPTER FIFTEEN

The Last Attack

PROFESSOR Miron Vovski was awarded the Order of Lenin, the highest Soviet decoration, in 1947. The citation spoke of 'heroic achievements during the fighting for Leningrad' during World War II. Vovski was a leading Soviet physician and one of the medical advisers of the Soviet leadership. His distinguished colleague Professor Vinigradov was awarded the Order of Lenin in 1952 for services in the field of medicine. He had given loyal service during the third Show Trial in connection with Yagoda's alleged poisonings.

The inconspicuous notice which appeared on the last page of *Pravda* on 13th January 1953 announcing the arrest of both Professors and seven other prominent members of the medical profession therefore came as a bolt from the blue. These 'Kremlin Doctors' were accused of bringing about the death of Politburo Member Andrei Zhdanov and of Colonel-General Shcherbakov by deliberately falsifying diagnosis and treatment. The nine doctors were also accused of attempting to kill a number of senior officers, among them Marshals Koniev, Govorov and Vasilevsky.

Five of the doctors were Jewish and according to the official announcement they had acted on the instructions of 'Joint', an international Jewish organisation. *Pravda*'s comments on the case read like quotations from the National-Socialist Press with their references to 'The Jewish world conspiracy'. Three of the doctors who were not Jews were said to have worked for the British Intelligence Service. Five of the others had also been given assignments by the CIA. A woman doctor, Lidya Timashuk, was awarded the Order of Lenin for discovering the plot.

The Security Services came in for much abuse for failing to discover these 'monsters, murdering doctors, abortions worthy of execration and despicable hirelings' in good time and overlooking 'their terrorist wrecking activities'.

The Security Services underwent a number of changes and re-organisations after the *Yezhovchina*. Yezhov himself was replaced at the end of the Great Purge by Lavrenti Beria. His further history is obscure. It is rumoured that he went mad. Other rumours have it that he was quietly liquidated when his work was finished. Stalin wrote in the 1947 edition of his *Problems of Communism:* 'Unfortunately more mistakes were committed than one could accept. There can be no doubt that we no longer need to apply the method of purges on a mass scale. Nevertheless, the purge carried out between 1933 and 1936 was essential and gave substantially positive results.' Zhdanov, Stalin's heir-apparent after the war, referred more explicitly to falsified evidence and stupid over-eagerness.

Beria started his career as a member of the NKVD in the Caucasus. He first comes to notice as the author of a history of the Party in Georgia which 'corrects' the accounts of other Party historiographers who did not give sufficient emphasis to Stalin's role. The NKVD expanded under his direction. In 1941 the Chief Administration of State Security (GUGB) became a separate People's Commissariat under Beria's Deputy, Merkulov, with Beria in general supervision. The two organisations were merged again at the outbreak of war, when Beria was made a Marshal of the Soviet Union, and finally divided in 1943. Both organisations now faced new and gigantic tasks: the entire population of the areas occupied by the Germans and reconquered must be thoroughly combed for unreliable and subversive elements, all traces of anti-Soviet attitudes must be eradicated, while the organisation itself needed an overhaul after the disruptions of war.

It might be thought that German wartime outrages would have eased the task of eliminating anti-Soviet and pro-German attitudes in the territories that they had occupied, but Soviet security files grew to mountainous proportions in the liberated areas. The entire population was divided into eight categories: partisans, patriots, neutrals, opportunists concerned only with their personal advantage, collaborators, provocationists, Gestapo agents, members of the Vlasov Army. Classification beyond 'neutral' meant deportation, beyond 'Gestapo agent' – execution. The fate of the Chechens, to mention only one ethnic group, shows that this system of classification could be extended to a whole people.

The end of the war required the creation of a new category for returning soldiers and for workers deported by the Germans. The image of the capitalist world which they brought back did not correspond in any way to that painted by Soviet propaganda.

Even the worst excesses of Nazism could not blind them to the fact that workers elsewhere in Europe were not dying of hunger as they had been told and that capitalism provided a standard of living undreamed of by the Soviet citizens. A sour joke of that period has it that Stalin made two mistakes: he showed Europe to the Red Army and the Red Army to Europe.

In 1946 the Security Services were once again reorganised to meet their growing commitments. All People's Commissariats were renamed Ministries; the MVD under Kruglov and the MGB under Abakumov were supplemented by the Ministry of State Control under the former Head of the NKGB, Merkulov. Beria, now a Deputy Prime Minister, was placed in general control of security matters.

The presence in the West of thousands of Soviet citizens, swept out of the country by the war and unwilling to return, created new and intractable problems for the Soviet authorities. These new émigrés were soon joined by a number of important defectors, such as Alexander Orlov, one time Head of the NKVD's transport organisation and later an adviser at the Soviet Embassy in Madrid during the Spanish Civil War, and the senior Soviet technologist Victor Kravchenko who wrote *I Chose Freedom*. These people were deeply implicated in the purges, having faithfully served the Soviet regime throughout the thirties, but their revelations opened the eyes of the world to the true nature of Soviet rule. And now, as Khrushchev put it at the Twentieth Party Congress: 'Stalin became even more moody, touchy, and cruel after the war. Above all, he became more distrustful. His persecution mania grew to unbelievable proportions. . . .'

Stalin was seventy-three when the arrest of the Kremlin Doctors heralded the beginning of yet another purge. It was a lonely old man who ruled the Communist half of the world: Milovan Djilas, then a close companion of Tito and a Yugoslav Communist leader, saw him early in 1948:

> I observed directly in front of me his already hunched back and the bony grey nape of his neck with its wrinkled skin above the stiff marshal's collar. I reflected: Here is one of the most powerful men of today, and here are his associates. . . .
> The dinner began with someone – it seems to me that it was Stalin himself – proposing that everyone guess how many degrees

below zero it was, and that everyone be punished by being made to drink as many glasses of vodka as the number of degrees he guessed wrong. . . . Such a beginning to the dinner forced upon me a heretical thought: These men shut up in a narrow circle were capable of inventing even more senseless reasons for drinking vodka – the length of the dining room in feet perhaps, or of the table in inches. And who knows, maybe that's what they do! At any rate, this apportioning of vodka glasses according to the temperature reading suddenly brought to my mind the confinement, the inanity and senselessness of the life the Soviet leaders were living, gathered round about their superannuated chief, even as they played a role that was decisive for the human race. . . .[1]

Stalin ruled the Soviet Empire from these closed Kremlin apartments surrounded by ghosts – millions of dead revolutionaries, Party leaders, marshals, generals and ministers, the purged of all nations, the deported, the shot and those who had starved and frozen to death. Yet Stalin could claim that he had won. He had overcome his opponents everywhere. He had achieved victory in the war after the Germans stood at the gates of Moscow and Leningrad. He had made the Russian imperial dream come true: Red Army men lined a frontier stretching from the 38th Parallel in Korea to the Brandenburg Gate in Berlin. Obedient viceroys, who could be thrown on the scrap-heap if they did not obey his orders to the letter, governed the East European Satellites on Moscow's behalf.

What caused this man, old but successful beyond all expectation, suddenly to discover another plot and to revive the evil memories of conspiracies and assassinations in Soviet minds? The answer may lie in Stalin's last work, *Economic Problems of Socialism in the USSR* published in October 1952, in which he repeatedly mentions foreign affairs:

Many Comrades assert that as a result of new conditions in the international field after the Second World War it is no longer inevitable that there should be wars between the capitalist countries. They consider that the contradictions between the Socialist Camp and the Capitalist Camp are stronger than the contradictions among the capitalist countries, that the United States of America have subjected the other capitalist countries to such an extent that they will not permit these countries to wage war on each other and mutually weaken each other. . . .

These Comrades are in error. . . . Let us take England and France first. They are undoubtedly imperialist countries. Cheap raw materials and secure markets are undoubtedly of first-rate importance to them. Can one really assume that they will tolerate the present situation indefinitely . . . when American capital draws the raw materials and the markets in the Anglo-French colonies to itself and thereby threatens to ruin the high profits of the Anglo-French?

Is it not more correct to say that capitalist England and after it capitalist France also will in the end be forced to tear themselves free from the USA's embrace. . . . . Let us now consider the main vanquished countries, Germany and Japan. These countries at present eke out a wretched existence under the heel of American imperialism. If one were to assume that these countries would not try to get to their feet again, that they would not try to break out of the US 'regime' and advance along the road of independent development, one would be prepared to believe in miracles. . . .

Divest this analysis of its Marxist-Leninist jargon and a clear picture emerges: former allies and former enemies will one day rebel against American domination. There will be a revolt in the capitalist camp just as there has been a revolt of the oppressed against the exploiters in the Soviet camp. Stalin used the Communist Parties to suppress the revolt of the nationalists and Terror to suppress the National Communists. The United States have no comparable resources at their disposal and the revolt of the oppressed must therefore inevitably lead to war.

One may wonder whether Stalin genuinely believed that war would break out within the capitalist camp, within a decade or so, if not immediately, and whether he planned to promote such a war or to hasten its outbreak so as to gain another chance of overrunning the rest of Europe. Be that as it may, it is the conclusions that Stalin drew from his forecast of world affairs which led to the renewal of the Terror.

This time the Terror was directed at the Soviet nation as a whole because it was beginning to relax after the horrors of the war and longing to live in greater ease, to be done with past austerities. Two hundred million people knew that they had beaten Hitler, destroyed Fascism and established Communism in Eastern Europe. They felt that they had earned the right not to freeze or go hungry any longer. It might even seem to some that a reversal of priorities as between heavy industry and the consumer goods industries should come as a matter of course. Only the threat of another war could restrain such dangerous desires.

New slogans made their appearance: 'Be vigilant! Be prepared! Victory is in danger!' These slogans were necessary in any event.

The international situation placed an ever-increasing strain on the resources of the Soviet Union. The Red Army was needed at full strength to hold down the occupied territories of Eastern Europe. Huge investments were essential to catch up with the Western lead in atomic techniques. The need to boost the economy of China, where the Communists had just come to power, imposed a heavy burden on the Soviet economy. Only Terror could restrain the unrest and dissatisfaction which these added burdens imposed on the Soviet population were certain to provoke.

The course of events after Stalin's death proves that this assessment of the situation in his later years is well founded. His successors were forced to work for a lessening in international tension before they could stimulate the production of consumer goods even to a limited extent and only then did it become possible to scale down the Terror. Similarly, the ideological rift with China is largely the result of the unwillingness or inability of the Soviet leaders to go on pouring resources into the Chinese economy without any likelihood of return. Stalin could not have taken this road even if he had wished to do so, because it leads away from Bolshevism, the ideological rule by violence of a minority over a whole people. Marx might have disagreed with the Chinese Communists when they branded Stalin's successors as revisionists, but Lenin would have supported them. In these terms a renewal of the Terror at the end of Stalin's reign was inevitable.

It is not clear what direction the last wave of the Terror launched by Stalin would eventually have taken, because he died too soon. Its beginnings, however, suggest that it was to be directed against every centrifugal tendency in the Soviet Union, against all those whose allegiance to Russia might not be whole-hearted or complete. For instance, in November 1951 a purge in Georgia eliminated 'nationalist' and 'terrorist' elements in the Party and the Government. Three Ministers lost their appointments and several thousand officials were arrested. The normal pattern of Stalin's purges required some prominent victims to start the process and it is no accident that when the Kremlin Doctors supplied this, part of them should have been Jews. Throughout the history of the West Jews have supplied the aliens in our midst who could be singled out for hatred, and anti-semitism is endemic among Russians. The creation of the State of Israel made many Jews in the Soviet Union look longingly away from the harsh realities of their condition towards the Promised Land and this fitted them even better to be the 'rootless cosmopolitans', whom Stalin required to point the need for Russians to close their ranks.

Intellectuals came under fire for the same reason. Their hopes of an easier life when the war was over included a wish for greater freedom to think and experiment. Their models lay abroad because all possible sources of new inspiration had been suppressed in the great drive for conformity during the past twenty years. They were both conspicuous and vulnerable, because intellectual and artistic activity must be communicated if it is not to die. And so the intellectuals joined the Jews as objects of persecution, cosmopolitans, subjectivists and budding petit-bourgeois.

By February 1953 the Soviet Press was in full cry and the Security Services were getting into their stride. The stream of forced confessions implicating an ever increasing number of people, no matter whether guilty or innocent, was back in fashion. A case from the time of *Yezhovchina* quoted by Wolfgang Leonhard illustrates the unreality and tragic absurdity of the process:

> Somebody confessed to being a member of a dangerous conspiracy against the Navy. He said that he and his friends had a plan to throw stones into the harbour at Kronstadt so as to sabotage the fleet and the naval installations. . . . He got eight years. If he had not confessed, he would probably have been sentenced to ten or twelve years. Besides, he was sure to be one of the first to be released when the whole case was reviewed as he hoped it would be.
>
> It was a fantastic, inconceivable situation. . . . We were witnessing responsible men who had never done anything against the system, solemnly and anxiously debating what they would confess after their arrest!

This was once again the atmosphere in the Soviet Union in February 1953. Stalin arranged that microphones should be concealed in Marshal Voroshilov's apartment. People like Molotov and Mikoyan considered the possibility of being arrested. According to a statement at the Nineteenth Party Congress two thousand posts were vacant in the Leningrad Party organisation alone. Khrushchev later claimed that several hundred officials, including some Ministers, were shot in the 'Leningrad Affair', the causes and details of which remain obscure to this day. It is not difficult to imagine the new heights that the Terror might have reached if Stalin had not died on 5th March 1953.

SOURCE
1. Milovan Djilas, *Conversations with Stalin* (Harcourt, Brace & World, New York, 1962).

CHAPTER SIXTEEN

The Way Back

ACCORDING to the official Soviet communiqué Stalin suffered a stroke on 3rd March 1953 and died at 21.50 two days later. His death was announced on 6th March.

Rumour and legend surround the death of all tyrants. Stalin's death was no exception. One story has it that he was knocked down during a stormy meeting of the Politburo and finished off with a poisoned drink, another that he was found unconscious at his villa outside Moscow and poisoned by Beria before he could recover. The announcement in *Izvestia* only two weeks before Stalin's death of the untimely demise of Major-General Kozynkin, Commander of the Kremlin Guard, on 15th February lent substance to the rumours. The truth may well never be known. All that need be said is that Stalin himself had created the circumstances in which such rumours inevitably flourished. He had isolated himself from his own people, he had surrounded himself with secrecy and he had put into mass production the systematic use of violence as an instrument of government. It is very fitting that the stories about his death should bear such a close resemblance to the official indictment of Yagoda, his own Security Service Chief, at the third Show Trial for poisoning Menzhinski, Gorky and Kuibyshev and to the accusation that the Kremlin Doctors had killed Zhdanov in the course of treatment.

Who can tell to what new heights the new wave of terror might not have reached if Stalin had not died when he did? In the past no purge was complete until it had implicated some member of the Communist leadership. As Khrushchev told the Twentieth Party Congress: 'One accepted a friendly invitation from Stalin and did not know where one would go afterwards – home or to prison.' And personal considerations apart, some members of the leadership must have recoiled before the prospect of yet another holocaust of people who desired only to live in peace.

In the book already quoted, Djilas provides Stalin's epitaph:

> Every crime was possible to Stalin, for there was not one he had not committed. Whatever standards we use to take his measure, in

any event – let us hope for all time to come – to him will fall the glory of being the greatest criminal in history. For in him was joined the criminal senselessness of a Caligula with the refinement of a Borgia and the brutality of a Tzar Ivan the Terrible.

Within a month of Stalin's death the rehabilitation of the Kremlin Doctors was officially announced. The statement mentioned the use of impermissible methods used to secure confessions which 'are strictly forbidden under Soviet law'. It is typical of the deviousness of Soviet practice and of the mystery that surrounds even the most public occasions in the Soviet Union that thirteen doctors were declared innocent while only nine had been mentioned in the original accusation. What is more, two of the latter are not among those rehabilitated. They may have died in custody or they may have collaborated too willingly with their interrogators – we shall probably never know.

The speed with which the rehabilitation was announced was a pointer to the eagerness of the new rulers to reassure the population. The proof that things changed came with the elimination of Beria. But the story of the Bolshevik Terror is not yet over. When Khrushchev blamed Stalin for the mass murder of millions he made it clear that all this had been unnecessary because by the time it happened the threat to the regime had been overcome. His meaning was clear: the 'extra-ordinary Mass Terror' could safely be kept in reserve, while 'ordinary Terror' remained the order of the day.

In 1954 a KGB officer, Nikolai Kokhlov, surrendered to the West German authorities and informed them that he had been assigned to murder the leader of a Russian émigré organisation with a gun concealed in a cigarette case and firing cyanide pellets. Eight years later another KGB agent was sentenced at Karlsruhe for the murder of two Ukrainian exiles by similar means. The habit of assassination for political reasons stretches back to the very origins of the Bolshevik movement and is by no means dead.

When the Hungarian people tried to rid themselves in 1956 of the intolerable burden of Communist tyranny, inefficiency and corruption they were crushed by the Soviet Army. In 1968, a movement of protest against the growing restrictions on independent thought and the senselessness of many official policies developed in Poland; it was suppressed by a purge and the authorities claimed that it had been instigated jointly by the Federal German Government and Zionist propaganda organisations, a most unlikely combination. Violence is still in order when the Communist system is threatened and the most unconvincing reasons will serve to launch a purge.

Within the Soviet Union itself modest demands for intellectual and artistic freedom and for the observance of constitutional rights have been answered by the increasing use of well tried Secret Police methods, officially inspired campaigns of slander and trials prepared in advance.

The Security machine has been scaled down and brought under better control, but it still exists. The principle of using Terror as an instrument of government lies at the very heart of the system invented by Lenin and perfected by Stalin. The choice before the Soviet rulers cannot be deferred much longer: to abandon Terror and thereby abandon Bolshevism, or to turn back into the dark and crush the aspirations of their own people. They would prefer to forget the necessity of this choice, to paper over the cracks for a little longer. But that can no longer be done – Czechoslovakia is now there to point the moral.

Index